THE VIEW FROM OVER THE HILL
Reflections on a life well misspent

by Steve Liddick

THE VIEW FROM OVER THE HILL
Reflections on a life well misspent

by Steve Liddick

DEDICATION

To my friends, Gloria Nagy-Wurman
and Bobbi Maass-Weinstein,

Other books by Steve Liddick:

Novels:
All That time
Old Heroes
Prime Time Crime
Sky Warriors

Cookbooks
Campsite Gourmet: Fine Dining on the Trail and on the Road
Eat Cheap: A Cookbook and Guide to Stretching Your Food Budget Dollars

Memoir:
But First This Message: A Quirky Journey in Broadcasting

Gift Book:
A Family Restaurant is No Place For Children: The Wit and Wisdom of an Uncommon Mom

THE VIEW FROM OVER THE HILL

I once told a friend I was over the hill and she said, "Now you'll pick up speed going down the other side."

Who am I to argue? After all, she's the one who gave me a Superman T-shirt.

Well, I may not be the man I used to think I was, but let's keep the illusion going, shall we?

In my 80-plus trips around the sun I've learned a few things, made some observations, and formulated some half-assed notions about life and the human condition—which I am happy to share with anyone kind enough to listen without dozing off.

Contained herein are some random reflections, philosophical meanderings, pet peeves, and comments on a lot of stuff one witnesses over a lifetime.

In my time above ground I have amused and offended a lot of people with my writing and my sparkling personality. I'm too old to change. If I started to behave myself now to get into Heaven under the wire, St. Peter would laugh his ass off and God wouldn't even put my application on His slush pile.

That said, I decided to write a book and continue my obnoxious ways.

Deal with it.

PILLS: THEIR FINAL DESTINATION

When we take a pill, how does the pill know where to go? I mean, you take an aspirin for a headache and it goes to your head. Right? Why doesn't it go, say, to your left elbow?

Even more confusing for me—if not for the pill—is how does a pill designed to reduce cholesterol distinguish itself from one created to treat an enlarged prostate or an irregular heartbeat? If you are taking both, do they fight it out in your stomach in a monster Pharma Smackdown?

Another thing (Oh, no . . . not *another* thing !!); should the pill taker take them one at a time or just slosh the entire daily array down in a single gulp? If they all go down in a mini tsunami, is there a mad scramble at the bottom to sort out which direction to take?

I'd like to think the drug companies worked out those details, but I sometimes wonder whether the mouse they tested the drug on survived and went on to live happily ever after, producing a new family every 20 days.

And here is something I also think about; why is it that a lot of the drugs advertised on television have a Z or X in their name? The ones I take do not have those consonants in their names and it concerns me. Am I getting the same full strength medication from Ragmopsiposian as I might get from ZaXahootinphloX?

Speaking of drugs advertised on TV, have you ever noticed that the disclaimer that follows claims of benefits takes up more than half of the commercial and is scarier than watching "Nightmare on Elm Street" by yourself in the dark.

You are cautioned that by taking this or that pill you risk impotence, ultra low blood pressure, bad breath, seizures, stinky feet, fiery rashes, and/or having dreams of showing up at a high school class reunion in your underwear.

The possible side effects are so frightening it makes the pill-taker feel that the disease or condition being treated is not nearly as dangerous as the cure.

3

Then the drug company absolves itself of any responsibility for the fiery hell they could be throwing your into by cautioning you to consult with your family physician before taking the medication.

Let that poor sap take the blame if everything goes south.

THE OTHER SIDE OF THE PLAYGROUND

When I was growing up, all efforts were made to keep the boys separate from the girls. At my elementary school there were even separate entrances for each. The girls couldn't play with the boys on the segregated playground pickup softball games. They might skin a knee or something awful like that.

It went on like that until high school. By that time separateness was pretty well established.

Adolescent boys had buddies, pals, homies, comrades described in various macho ways. Bruises were common. Spitting was encouraged. Belching was a competitive sport.

Adolescent girls had girlfriends and phoned each other every evening to ask what the other was going to wear to school the next day. They had pencil boxes with drawers that contained a ruler, a protractor, and a big rubber eraser. Every pencil was sharpened.

They had circled their wagons into cliques dedicated to delicate activities in which they would not skin their knees or something awful like that.

The upshot is that by the time we hit our teens we didn't really know much about the opposite sex. How could we? The boys were always over here wearing blue; the girls were always over there in their pinks.

So, there I was at 17 with some mysterious force at work drawing me to this group of total strangers. What's a poor hormone-saturated teenager to do? Woe is me. Know what I'm saying?

To make a long story a little longer, we worked it out. Clumsily, I admit. Lots of kicking the dirt and blushing and finally getting around to asking one of those alien beings on a date.

It became a little less clumsy as time went by. We learned the rules: don't honk your horn at the curb when you pick up your date; say nice things about her mother and, when discussing what time she is to be home, never tell her father you'll have her in bed by ten.

Sure, we got better at sorting out the gender differences, but the truth is, a lot of the mystery never did go away.

The years went by. We got married, continued to work at trying to figure out the other half, some of us failed monumentally, divorced, and went our separate ways.

When I got suddenly single at 38, it wasn't much different from when I was 17. Again there was an entire world of semi-strangers out there.

I'm married again. Got a good one this time. Or maybe it was I who became better. Hard to say.

I don't kid myself that I have entirely figured out the pink half of the species. But I learned a couple of tricks to avoid trouble.

Saying "I'm sorry" goes a long way toward domestic tranquility.

Saying "yes dear," usually takes care of the rest.

ADDICTED TO OUR iPHONES

We are becoming a nation of addicts. I don't mean drugs, although that is another problem to discuss at another time. No, we are becoming addicted to our iPhones.

You see it all the time; mostly young people walking down the street talking on their cell phones, seemingly unaware of the world around them. I have seen people walk into lamp posts and parking meters—even into other people.

Occasionally you see couples in restaurants or two people walking side by side, talking on their phones, not conscious of the actual human next to them. You have to wonder who they are talking to. Possibly each other, but they apparently don't know how to relate in the old-fashioned face-to-face mode.

I went to a county fair once and saw a young woman sitting on her horse, completely oblivious to her surroundings and—I'm not making this up—she was texting. It was as though the horse was not even there, just a convenient place to sit. At the very least she might have taken her weight off the poor animal and found a conventional chair to do her texting.

More and more car crashes these days involve drivers who were texting instead of paying attention to the road ahead of them. Texting while driving is every bit as dangerous as driving drunk.

I own an iphone, of course. It would be un-American not to. I'm not addicted to it, though. I only use it for phone calls, email, messaging friends, connecting to the Internet, reading my Kindle books, checking Facebook, Twitter, Instagram, and LinkedIn, monitoring my checking account, watching TV shows and movies on Amazon Prime, Netflix, Hulu, and Crackle, taking pictures, checking Craigslist, ordering items through Amazon, and as a calculator. I don't wear a watch anymore, so I also use the phone to give me the time, to remind me when to walk the dog, water the outdoor plants, take my pills, and carry the trash down to the road for weekly pickup.

But I it's not like I'm addicted or anything. Like today's young people.

THE WORLD'S GREATEST INVENTION

There are conflicting views as to what is the greatest invention in all of mankind. Some argue that it is the printing press. Others nominate the wheel. The transistor gets a lot of votes.

Oh, sure, you can make the case for safety pins, the Roomba, and the spittoon, but I personally believe one of man's creations stands above them all. And that is—the erasable pen.

A pen whose ink can be erased serves several purposes: (1) you can go back over your crossword puzzle answers when you make a mistake and not have a bunch of smudges on it so you come off looking like a doofus, and (2) You can proudly say, "I do the New York Times crossword puzzle in *ink*." How often that we can we brag about such a monumental achievement?

I would say 'I rest my case,' but wait—there's more.

How about the crossword puzzle, itself. Someone sat down and worked it out in their own head. Probably the same genius who invented origami and who had enough spare time on his hands to get the puzzle job done and give people all over the world a chance to find out they don't know everything.

This would be an invaluable lesson for teenagers.

Is there any better therapy for the brain—mental gymnastics, if you will—than working on the daily brain teaser? No better aid for the elderly has ever been conceived. And that includes the adult diaper.

Exercising the brain is no less important than exercising the body. With crossword puzzles you don't even have to get up out of your easy chair to do it.

On the flip side of benefits for the elderly, there is aggravation in the young who have not had enough time in life to accumulate information—especially stuff from way back when—because they weren't there way back then. That is important to know because, when the puzzlemaker asks for actress _____ Davis (five letters), and a young whippersnapper writes in "Geena," they darn well better have an erasable pen handy because the puzzle is probably looking for "Bette."

Okay, now I do rest my case.

LADY LUCK SNARLS AT ME

Not only did we not have all of the numbers in the recent Mega Gazillion dollar lottery jackpot, we did not have *any* of the numbers. What are the odds of that?

They say that you can't win if you don't play, but the chances of not winning even if you *do* play are astronomical.

We often hear that statistically you have a better chance of being struck by lightning than winning the lottery. That is especially true in my case because I guarantee that if I go outside during an electrical storm, I am, literally, toast.

My bad luck mojo only relaxed its grip on me one time. It was at a roller skating party in 1953. A drawing was held and I won a stuffed duck. I should have had that duck bronzed because it was the last time Ms. Luck smiled on me.

Years ago I had a friend who would play the pinball machines regularly. The games cost five cents in those days. That guy could get more out of a nickel than anyone I know. He routinely won so many games that he never spent more than a quarter. I am confident that before I would win a single pinball game, that machine would collapse from the weight of the nickels I had to put into it.

The same guy also had a lot of luck with the ladies. Well, I'm no George Clooney, but that guy got hit with an ugly stick and the girls still fell all over him.

I should mention that my lucky friend's luck ran out when he was relatively young.

I'm still above ground and I still don't play the pinball machines.

There is a saying that "what goes up must come down." Well, I never bounce on a trampoline because I don't want to take any chances.

AT WAR WITH MY WARDROBE

It's funny how perspective changes over a lifetime. When I was ten-years-old I thought nothing of walking two miles to Tommy's Ice Cream Parlor for a cherry milkshake. Today I give careful thought to whether or not I'll even get up off my easy chair and walk to the kitchen for a diet Coke.

It's that way with whatever I'm wearing, too. There was a time when I would practically fling clothes on myself without any thought and race out of the house. Today, what should be the simple act of putting on a pair of socks could easily be compared to calisthenics.

I know my feet are down there somewhere beyond the flab and the aching joints. I'm just having trouble coordinating mind and body, which is further complicated by the addition of the socks. Joints don't really bend in the direction you need them to in order to twist one's body around to get two socks over ten toes that are dead set against receiving them.

A pair of pants offers a similar challenge; two legs on the human, two legs on the pants. Tab A, Slot A. Repeat with Tab B. Simple, right? Well, I don't know how it is with you kids, but this old geezer has to hold onto something to get the job done. Even then it is a struggle to coordinate the extremities with the target while hopping around the room tugging, bouncing, straining, and trying to avoid falling down.

I find that swearing is no help at all. That never stops me, of course.

And here's another thing ("Oh, no, not another thing"). There was a time when the space between the ringing of the alarm clock and my walking out the door was almost too short a span to measure. Fast forward to present day and I am here to tell you that if I still had to go to a 9 to 5 job I would have to start my preparation at 4 a.m.

In addition to the standard morning routine—which is difficult enough in and of itself—there is the pills and eye drops regime, plus all the appliances one must locate and install: glasses—which I often have a hard time finding without my glasses—hearing aids . . . yadda, yadda.

Not to mention the aforementioned time-consuming, energy-devouring getting dressed part of the ritual.

Thank God I don't have a wooden leg or I'd never get out of here.

STICKERS ON FRUIT

Have you ever wondered why there are stickers on fruit sold in supermarkets? Those usually include the name of the company that sold the fruit to the grocery chain, along with a picture of the item, itself, It's pretty obvious that a banana is a banana and a pear is a pear without attaching a picture of it to tell you what it is sticking on.

The fruit was probably grown by some poor farmer, possibly in a third world country, who invested money and labor, and risked pests, drought, fire, and the wrath of God to grow what sits in a basket in your kitchen or dining room.

Then the middleman came along and took ownership, slapped a sticker on the fruit, shipped it to market, and took all the credit.

I have several objections to the practice. Objection 1: I don't need to be told what is so obvious. Objection 2: I don't care who caused said fruit to get to my supermarket. Objection 3: You can't get the #%& sticker off the fruit without damaging it.

Pardon my language.

Years ago, when I worked at a Los Angeles radio station I wondered aloud in a newscast why the U.S. Postal Service used wimpy glue on the back of stamps that ensured that the stamp would come off if even slightly moistened while in transit. I suggested that postal officials should consider partnering with the creators of bumper stickers so they could make stamps that would stay stuck. Those #%& bumper stickers *never* come off.

Again, pardon my language.

Years later the postal service, whether having heard of my suggestion or simply put two-and-glue together on their own, adopted the bumper sticker idea with their stamps.

We all know that government is slow to act, if it acts at all. But you have to wonder why it took them centuries to realize the need to improve their stickum.

I leave you with this suggestion: Never put a U.S. Postal Service stamp on your vehicle's bumper because those #%& things will never come off.

Oops!

WHO SAYS CEMETERIES ARE QUIET PLACES?

When the county planning commission held a hearing to listen to any objections to the creation of a cemetery adjacent to our acreage, we attended. For many years before that, cattle grazed next door. We often reached across the fence between us to scratch a Brahma bull on the forehead. I enjoyed the experience and I assume the bull did, too.

But we knew that when planning commissions meet to hear objections from neighbors about anything, the fix is already in. The decision has already been made. The hearing is being held so they can say they held a hearing.

It was approved, of course.

Okay, how much trouble can a cemetery be? Dead people are well known for being a quiet lot.

Little did we know.

We forgot about visitors, lawn maintenance equipment, grave-digging machinery, dumpster pickup and delivery trucks, electric water pumps, noisy mufflers, and mourners who bring their loud children with them. In the nearly ten years since the cemetery started there has been a constant din coming across the fence between us.

The live-in maintenance man has a car alarm that goes off day or night. I ask you, why does a car alarm have to be so sensitive? Also, why do you have to even set your car alarm in a—for pete's sake—cemetery? Who's gonna steal it? In all these years I have never seen a single zombie car thief.

Just our luck, the master bedroom in our house is at the cemetery end and the alarm often goes off in the middle of the night.

Winds here typically blow from the south. The cemetery is south of us. Wind-blown debris from graves routinely finds its way onto our property; plastic flowers, balloons, pinwheels, flower wrapping papers, and wrappers from candy and fast food items that people—for reasons that baffle me—bring with them. A cemetery would not seem to me to be a preferred dining place.

If the star of the funeral is a person of status, it is not uncommon for hundreds of people to show up to mourn—or to be sure he's dead. They bring their cars with them, of course, and many of them park those cars along both sides of the busy narrow road bordering our land, blocking through traffic. Many of those cars are parked in front of our mailbox and between the "No Parking Between Signs" signs. On several occasions, cars were parked right in our lane, which is clearly a lane.

We have nearly a thousand neighbors next door to us who never make a sound. But those they left behind sure are a noisy bunch.

It would do no good to complain because, unlike cities, there are no county noise regulations out here in the sticks, and I know of nowhere that rudeness is against the law, although it should be.

When I'm King things are really going to be different around here.

WHEN I GROW UP

I think we can all agree that until we were at least into our late 20s, early 30s most of us—typically the male half of the human species—were not as mature as we should be. Some never got over it.

In our teen years we liked to think we knew everything. Actually, we believed that everything we knew *was* everything—and our parents were idiots.

It is beyond me how we could possibly have continued to have confidence that we were all-knowing if we kept making stupid decisions. That alone should have been a clue about how little experience we had to do the right things.

The crossword puzzles are a good example. Even the smartest little kid can't possibly do the New York Times crossword puzzle. They haven't had enough experience or education in their unformed brains with the information it takes to fill in a puzzle's squares. It's like that with everything else in our lives. Inputting data is what makes the difference.

If you were absent from elementary school the week your class learned how to do addition in their heads, there is a serious vacuum in your math education. You'll be counting on your fingers for the rest of your life.

Missing links come in other forms, too—where you have to know one thing in order to learn the next higher level up the chain: the alphabet to make words, words to make sentences, sentences to make paragraphs—and then everything else you need to know.

I wonder if parents today read to their kids and get them interested in finding out about the world through books.

Mother Goose, the Brothers Grimm, Aesop, and Dick, Jane, and Sally are critical links in the chain of knowledge. Although we can never hope to know everything, reading is a good start on learning what we need to know.

If I don't know anything else, of this I am absolutely certain.

WHEN FRUIT TASTED LIKE FRUIT

A century or so ago, when I was a just kid, my Grandmother always had a bowl of fruit on the dining room table. The apples were the crispest, sweetest ever plucked from a tree. The pears were so juicy, you had to lean forward to keep from dribbling onto your clothes. Cherries, grapes, and plums made your taste buds sing.

Today, when you go to the supermarket, the fruit is rock hard, not even close to ripe. It was taken from the tree while still green. If it had been ripe and soft when picked, it would be bruised by the time it bounced around on a bumpy truck and reached the consumer. Nobody would buy something as ugly as that. Most fruit sold today would not ripen in Grandma's bowl. It has to get its final magic right on the tree for full flavor.

We're just too darned far from that tree. As a result, Americans have a very different idea of how good fruit can be.

For some time I thought the difference in taste might be because the older we get, the more of our taste buds go dormant. That theory was put to rest a few years ago when there was a sudden glut on the California pear market. A strike by the pickers slowed down picking—and picked up flavor. The supermarkets were flooded with pears that were actually ripe, juicy and—wait for it—tasted like the good old days. So, it wasn't my dying taste buds, after all.

Grandma would have been pleased.

LOOKING BACK AT LOOKING FORWARD

There were just 23 of us in my high school graduating class of 1955. It was a small rural district. Only 145 students in the entire school, grades eight through twelve. Farm kids mostly. A few townies.

As we sat in our homeroom in the last minutes of the last day of the last year of our high school career, we came face-to-face with the reality that this was the eve of the first day of the rest of our lives.

While waiting for the final dismissal bell, our homeroom teacher, Mr. Cornish, said, "You may not have thought about it, but this is probably the last time all of you will be together in one place."

What was on most of our minds just then was getting the (bleep) out of there, but I did have a sad moment thinking I would probably never again see some of these people I had gotten to know over the years.

One of the girls was saying she had no idea what she was going to do now. This was in an era when "housewife" was the major female occupation. I believe "secretary" ranked second and "tool factory" and "carpet mill worker" were high on the list.

As for myself, I knew exactly what I would be doing for the rest of my life. I had been the county news photo stringer for the city newspaper for several years. I knew for sure I was going to follow the photography career, eventually work for Life Magazine and win fame and fortune for my work.

So much for youthful optimism. Four years later I had abandoned photography for a career in radio, which I followed for the rest of my working life. I don't know what happened to the girl who didn't know what she was going to do, but I suspect that whatever it was she probably did it all the way to Social Security.

In the years since then I have not seen some of those people at all. I've been to a couple of class reunions and I am still in touch with several classmates. On one trip back to my hometown after a twenty-year absence, one of the 'girls' invited our fellow schoolmates to her home for a get-together. Eighteen showed up.

Eighteen of 23. Not bad. I believe that is equal to the best-attended formal reunion in the years since.

The Class of '55 has met every five years since graduation. Some of the gang even get together every couple of months for breakfast at a local restaurant, and that is well-attended, too.

We were a good group then and have gotten to know each other even better, as well as their spouses, children and grandchildren.

The nice people are still the nicest of the bunch. The grouches are still grouchy, but we like them anyway. As we faced the trials of growing up and growing old, we have become more understanding of how the grouches got that way because we are at least a little grouchy ourselves at times. No life goes without scars.

We've never seen some of that old gang because the high school experience didn't mean as much to them as to others; some because it was too much trouble or too expensive to dress up for a night out among people they never really got to know.

We are in our 80s now and our number has dwindled to 18. I think of Mr. Cornish's words occasionally, that we will never all get together in one place again.

It makes me a little sad, but it was a great time while it lasted.

COPING WITH "OFF" DAYS

Ever have one of *those* days? You know the kind of days I'm talking about. The ones where everything seems to go wrong and your brain appears to have turned to tapioca.

I had one of those days yesterday.

It began with waking up and trying to find my glasses. They were not on my nightstand where I put them the night before. I always get up way before dawn, so it was dark, I couldn't turn on my reading lamp because I didn't want to wake my wife. No matter, even with the light on I wouldn't be able to find my glasses without my glasses.

I assumed one of the cats knocked them off the stand, so I got down on my hands and knees on the floor to feel around for them. Found them—and the slippers that had also been moved.

The next challenge was to get back on my feet. No small matter for the chronically wobbly. I've considered installing a lifting device on the bedroom ceiling similar to the winches you see on the front of some pickup trucks.

Could this day get any worse?

Just wait.

I had bought a garden hose a few days earlier. When I got home I discovered that I already had a hose like the one I bought. So I drove to the garden store to ask for a refund. When I got there I realized I had forgotten my wallet. Without my wallet I couldn't get the refund charged back to my debit card—which I didn't have because I had forgotten the aforementioned wallet.

Could this day *possibly* get any worse?

Never ask that question because it absolutely can.

I drove on to the post office to pick up my mail and to send off my friend Barney's birthday card. The problem is, I had forgotten put a stamp on the card before I left home.

Remember the wallet I forgot and couldn't get a refund on the garden hose? I wasn't carrying any cash. I couldn't buy a stamp. It would have to wait until tomorrow.

To top it off, there was no mail. I had driven the seven miles to the post office for absolutely nothing—not even one lousy flyer

25

advertising something I didn't need, couldn't afford, or wouldn't use even if I got one as a gift.

Could this day possibly get . . . never mind.

Having undeniable recent experience with a day where things kept getting worse, I drove home cautiously. Miraculously, I got there without requiring the services of Triple-A, nor was I struck by an asteroid.

Not taking any chances, I spent the rest of the day on my lounge chair.

.

A TRADITION CORRUPTED

I am not a baseball fan or, for that matter, any kind of sports fan. But some traditions cry out to be upheld, regardless of their realm.

I'm talking about what may be the waning days of the revered Louisville Slugger baseball bat.

When someone hits a ball with a wooden bat, it is supposed to go "Whack!" Everyone on the field and in the stands knows that an American tradition has been upheld with the summer sound of ash on leather, just as God intended.

But not on today's Little League diamonds across the land. When we hear a collision of club and ball today it is the wimpy "Tink" of a bat made of—it pains me to say it—*aluminum*.

I put the blame squarely on the shoulders of Alcoa company marketers. I'm certain that some executive with no stake in the "Great American Pastime" decided that baseball bats made of aluminum would add significantly to the company's bottom line, so it is off to the dumpster with tradition, culture, and the-way-things-have-always-been.

Foiled again! Get it? Foiled—never mind.

Now I'm not generally a conspiracy theorist, but it seems to me that this could very well be another case of commerce corrupting tradition. You see it all the time: Crackerjack popcorn prizes of plastic and paper instead of tin and imagination; tearing down charming old buildings to build taller, cheaper, characterless structures that will, themselves, be torn down in a few years.

Thanks goodness Alcoa isn't in the iron business or using their baseball bats would cancel out the need for steroids to bulk up ballplayers.

But, as I said, I probably don't have a legitimate say in what baseball teams choose to bat their balls with since I m not a sports fan.

Well, maybe female mud wrestling.

27

A ROSE IS A ROSE—OR IS IT?

Remember when roses smelled like roses? They don't seem to do that anymore. I can't imagine why the aroma has been bred out of them. Or maybe I should say the appearance has been bred into them at the cost of that wonderful rose smell.

Without a doubt there are some beautiful roses out there. Some people make an entire career out of creating new varieties of the flower. They compete for prizes and—more important—to sell the rights to their creations to the big distributors for big bucks. Nothing wrong with that if you don't mind messing with Mother Nature.

But looks aren't everything.

Think back to high school. Did the prettiest girls and handsomest boys also have great depth of character? The ones who looked the best often figured they already were everything they had to be. Everyone told them how wonderful they were—and who were they to disagree? No need to do anything more than just sit there and be everything people said they were.

I think it may be like that in the rose business. Go for the looks; ditch the character.

For my part in it, just give me an old fashioned rose that fills the room with its essence.

I wonder what those majorettes and football heroes look like today.

29

DEALING WITH PAIN

I couldn't give you an accurate count of the number of times I've looked down at a hand or knee and discovered I've got a cut, scrape, or bruise and have no clue as to how it got there.

Not that I'm impervious to pain, so you would think I'd notice if I banged myself up.

I remember when my mother would announce that she had a headache. It never failed that my father would say, "so do I." And then she'd say "Dear God, the only pain I've ever been allowed to suffer alone is the pain of bearing my children." He couldn't top that one. The worst headache in the world has to be pretty puny compared to the pain of having a baby. I bet that hurts a lot.

Anyway, yesterday I got an injury that is no mystery. I was pruning the mulberry tree next to our back porch. When I squeezed the handles of the lopper, it slipped and I bunged up a knuckle pretty good against the rough bark of the tree. That hurt right away and I absolutely knew where, when, and how it happened.

When you have quite a few years behind you, you are sure to have piled up some aches and pains. It comes with the territory. I don't know how other people handle it, but I compartmentalize it. I put it in the background and ignore it. Mostly. If someone were to ask me if I hurt, I'd have to think about it. The answer would be "yes," of course, but it doesn't occupy my thoughts from moment to moment.

I didn't mention my skinned knuckle to my wife because I didn't want her to think I was being a baby. She has arthritis pretty bad. So, if you want to talk about pain, Sherry is an expert in that department.

Besides, I have not turned into my father, I don't care what my aunts say.

TOO TERRIBLE TO CONSIDER

I had a scary thought. What if everyone had already sold or given away all of their used stuff and there were no more yard sales and thrift stores because there was nothing left to be sold or donated?

First of all, my friend Mike would have a nervous breakdown. Then a national day of mourning would be declared to observe the junque vacuum. Flags at half staff.

How would people furnish their homes? Where would they get nick-nacks to fill every flat space in their houses? How could they possibly replace their cat-scratched sofas and their small appliances? If anyone wanted to read a book they would either have to get it from the library or—God forbid—buy it new. I can't even imagine that. A paperback book should cost a quarter, as God intended. A hard cover book should cost no more than a dollar.

The only books that should be allowed to be sold at full retail price are those bought directly from the publisher—and those I have written.

Publishers would be overjoyed to be charging full price, of course, but petroleum company executives would be outraged. Gas consumption would be down because millions of scavengers would no longer be driving around weekends looking for valuable art and artifacts to take to Antiques Road Show and get disgustingly rich.

You can't have people driving less. Oil executives' mansions cost money, you know. Tuition at top universities for their kids doesn't come cheap. Who's going to pay boarding and training fees for their race horses? Do you have any idea the psychological damage that would be done to be forced to give up their company jets—and golf? Have you no sympathy? Have you no humanity?

But wait. It just occurred to me that such a horrifying scenario can never occur as long as my friend Mike and I are alive. Between the two of us we already have enough junque to supply every yard sale and thrift store in America.

UNWELCOME VISITORS

A family of skunks has taken up residence under our garden shed; Mama Skunk, Papa Skunk, and three little stinklings.

My wife, Sherry, was the first to see them, although there was already a certain air in the neighborhood to announce their presence.

Don't get me wrong, we pretty much welcome all creatures great and small and skunks are said to be a sweet and gentle animal. There is that one thing about them, though.

Chip the Wonder Dawg goes nuts when he sees anything moving around on the other side of his backyard fence. I'm just hoping the skunks ignore his barking and don't unleash their superpower on him. That would not be good for Chip and it certainly would not be good for us if he got zapped and then came into the house.

I'm not sure if they are still here. Skunks are typically nomadic and usually migrate twice a year. But I still look around when I walk out that way, as though checking for renegade Indians. I don't want to surprise one of them—and be unpleasantly surprised in return.

We pretty much have a live-and-let-live attitude about critters. After all, they and their fellow species were here long before we were. Our philosophy is that when you build a house in the middle of a field, you should expect to occasionally have to deal with field creatures. We have been visited by mice, rats, gophers, moles, voles, possum, geese, raccoons, coyotes, owls, crows, hawks, rabbits galore, and the occasional King or Garter snake. We even had a pair of the neighbor's peacocks stop by a few years ago and roost on our roof before moving on. Hearing them walking around up there was kind of creepy, but we enjoyed their company. Even their occasional piercing scream that sounded like some kind of jungle beast.

I'll continue to walk carefully in the back yard for awhile, just in case I'm wrong about skunks being nomads.

A RELUCTANT TROOPER

It was 1961 and I was a U.S. Army private caught up in the big Vietnam era draft.

Our ship was headed for Korea where I was to be a radio announcer for the American Forces Korea Network (AFKN). The trip across the Pacific Ocean would take 30 days. The crossing on the USS General Edwin D. Patrick troop transport ship blazed along at seven knots—about the same speed as your average jogger.

To this day I still can't see how the government could believe it was cost-efficient to slowly transport a thousand troops across the Pacific Ocean on a ship. We were consuming three meals a day on a fuel-burning ship for an entire month. If my math is correct: 1000 men X 30 days = 30,000 days, divided by 365 days in a year = more than 80-years of our collective military service being wasted rather than working at the jobs we were ripped out of our civilian lives to perform. It seemed to me then and now that it would have been cheaper to fly us all there.

I had not yet been in the army long enough to realize that (a) logic has no place in the military (b) I must never question a decision made by anyone with a higher rank than mine, and (c) *everyone* was of a higher rank than mine.

Several weeks into the trip we were given a brief shore leave at Yokohama, Japan.

Japan is an ancient land brimming with tradition. One tradition among taxi drivers is that no matter where an American GI says he wants to go, he is driven to a part of town where the cab stops in front of a restaurant owned by the driver's cousin. Plus, on the way there the driver weaves in and out of traffic at terrifying speeds which no one in that pre-seatbelt and airbag era could possibly survive in the event of a crash. All this is done on the opposite side of the road from where we are accustomed to driving in America.

After several hours of walking up and down streets ablaze with neon lights, it was back to the ship and another taxi ride from hell.

Fast forward to a year later and time to return to the states.

Departure day arrived. I gathered up my gear and packed a crate of personal items to be shipped home. I said my goodbyes and rode a bus to Seoul.

I boarded the USS General J. C. Breckenridge troop ship at Inchon for the trip home.

When we arrived at Treasure Island, across the bay from San Francisco a month later we were herded into a huge warehouse and each given a checklist. The list itemized the various stations we were to stop at to turn in equipment, bring our medical and service records up to date, and be paid up to date.

After stopping at a half-dozen or so processing stations I must have looked puzzled as I poured over my checklist to see whether I had covered everything.

"Where are you supposed to be, young man?" asked an officer.

I said, "I'm not sure, sir."

He took my checklist and looked it over.

He handed the list back to me. "Son," he said, "you are out of the army."

Those were some of the sweetest words I had ever heard. They ranked way up there with the time Patty Sweeney said, "could you unzip me?"

OLD DOGS – NEW TRICKS

I'm considering starting a new business. I have a lot of time on my hands in my retirement, so I thought I would offer a service for people who have neither the time, the expertise, nor a digital camera and the knowledge of how to use it.

My service would be ideal for technophobes and those who are unskilled at the inner workings of a computer, the complexities of cyberspace in general, and the Internet in particular.

I propose to set up a Facebook page in their name, take pictures of their restaurant meals and post them on the site on their behalf.

Wait, don't laugh. We see such photos posted all the time by those lucky enough to own a digital camera, who are skilled at Facebook postings, and who dine out regularly.

But what of those poor souls who have restaurant meals that go unshared and unpublicized simply because they have no technical talents. Perhaps those poor unfortunates have an elderly flip phone with no photo capability? It is entirely possible that they have no nine-year-old child or grandchild to chauffeur them through the cyber world and unsnarl their computer for them if they even have a computer.

Wouldn't it be a valuable service to assist in putting those yummy meal images out there to be admired by Facebook "friends" and, at the same time, lessen the isolation they must surely feel by being left out?

A senior discount would be offered and a bulk rate would be available for those who eat out a lot.

SCOLDED WITH CLASS

After high school l moved to St. Petersburg, Florida. St. Pete was the springtime home of the New York Yankees and St. Louis Cardinals. The Cards spring training camp was at Al Lang Stadium, a miniature version of Yankee Stadium. The Yankees trained at Miller Huggins field, which looked a lot like the ball field from the later movie, *'Field of Dreams',* but without the cornfield. That puny practice facility would eventually cause the Yankees to leave town. The New York Mets replaced them at Miller Huggins.

As a newspaper photographer I covered everything from afternoon society ladies' teas to yacht races to sports. My sports coverage experience at a Pennsylvania newspaper just after I graduated from high school had prepared me well for photographing baseball.

In a baseball town, I was King Midas.

With no interest in sports beyond the action I was able to capture in my camera, here I was mingling with such baseball luminaries as Stengel, Berra, Mantle, Ford, Maris and Musial. Those were names I knew well because of all the hours I had spent hearing my grandfather talk about them as I sat next to him on the sofa while he yelled at the radio, telling them how the game should be played.

No one should ever doubt that professional ballplayers put as much effort into spring training games as they put into league games. Based on one experience I had with Stan "The Man" Musial that was certainly true.

Photographers covered baseball in two ways. One was a birds-eye view from high in the press box with a camera equipped with a monster telephoto lens. The other was my favored position, down on the field at first base.

The on-field photographer is about 15-feet from first, sighting down the base line to second, with a good view of third. If anything photogenic happened at any of the three, the cameraman was in the perfect spot to catch it and could also run to home plate if that is where the money shot was.

41

If nothing was going on at second or third, the photographer moved to about 15-feet from first base, sighting down toward home plate. There he waited for the batter to do something spectacular.

That was where I was standing when the bases were empty and Stan Musial came up to bat.

Musial hit a long fly ball deep into center field as I waited in the hope of getting a shot of the superstar in a picturesque slide or a close tag. Instead, the center fielder was set up to catch the ball and there was no need for the runner to hurry. But nobody told Musial. He was steaming toward the bag with all the gusto as if he had hit it out of the park—and nearly ran into me.

He came to a stop and walked over to me. He put his hand on my shoulder, walked me off to the side and said very gently, "It would be best if you stood off the baseline when the runner is likely to overrun the base."

I had never been scolded with such class in my life. Rather than embarrassment, I felt admiration. That small incident summed up the entire man and explained the affection fans had for him.

Musial was 40-years-old in 1960 and still turning in respectable performances. At the same time, John F. Kennedy was 43-years-old and campaigning for the presidency. It was said that Kennedy was too young to run and Musial was too old to run. Musial fooled them, though. He played three more seasons and retired the same year JFK was assassinated.

WOULD YOU PLEASE REPEAT THAT

My mother, my sister and I visited the Franklin Institute science museum in Philadelphia when I was nine or ten years old. Among the hands-on scientific exhibits was one where a man administered hearing tests. You would go into a soundproof booth, put on earphones and he would play sounds in varying decibel and tonal ranges. I scored exceptionally well, able to hear things very few people could detect.

In the early days of television I would walk into a room with a TV set and hear a high-pitched whistle that no one else ever seemed to notice. I mentioned that to the sound man. He said, "your hearing is far better than most people now, but when you get older, your hearing will be worse than most."

He was right on target with that prediction. In my early 40s I developed tinnitus—ringing in the ears that drowns out a lot of other sounds.

Once, when I pulled out an old audio tape of an interview with singers Johnny Cash and June Carter that I had done for Armed Forces Radio in Korea, the voices sounded mushy. I attributed it to the tape being a half century old and thought no more about it.

I often had to ask my wife to speak up. She does have a tiny voice in a low range and I figured that was the reason I had trouble hearing her. She kept telling me I should get checked.

I finally did.

Apparently getting older was enough to diminish my ability to hear. On top of that was years of having music blasting through my earphones in radio stations I worked in as a deejay, including the radio stations in Korea where there was no volume control on the earphones and the sound was much too loud. That was the beginning of the end of my hearing superpower.

For the past nine years I have worn hearing aids. My wife's voice is still tiny and in a low range, but I don't have to ask her to repeat as often.

I want to play that Johnny Cash-June Carter audio tape again to see if it sounds any better than the last time.

43

MOM SCARED MY BARBER

I was just out of high school and had a job in the city. I was feeling like I had left childhood behind, even though I was still living at home on the farm with the folks.

It's one of those points in a person's life where they believe they are entitled to start making some grownup decisions on their own.

For all of my life until then I had a full head of curly hair. While some may admire curly hair, I am here to tell you that it is the curls, not the owner of the head, that decide which way the hair will curl.

For the first several years of my life I had *red*, curly hair. I say without fear of contradiction that I was a beautiful child. I can say that now because all that soon went away.

My mother loved my curly hair and insisted that I keep it just the way it had always been. I hated it. I got tired of aunts and church ladies fluffing up my hair and making embarrassing comments. It didn't impress girls my age, but I had not yet gotten to the age where I cared what girls my age thought about my hair—or anything else.

By the time I got interested in what girls thought about me, the red in the hair had turned to brown, the curls were sticking out uncontrollably all over my head, and I had seriously and permanently gotten over being cute.

I decided to get a flattop haircut, the craze of the day. But I knew Mom would have a fit if my beloved curls ended up on the barbershop floor.

Well, I may not have been beautiful any more, but I was pretty clever and I devised a plan to change Mom's mind.

"Red" Stoops was the barber in my hometown. Like all small towns, everyone knew everyone and Red was no exception.

"I want a "Don Eagle" haircut, I told Red. Don Eagle was a professional TV wrestler with a strip of hair in the middle of his head from brow to nape. All the rest on the sides was shaved off.

"You want to get me killed, don't you," Red said. "Because if I gave you a haircut like that your mother would murder me."

The next time Red saw Mom he mentioned my request. She agreed that he had made the right decision and would remain in good health.

"What were you thinking," she said to me later.

"Well, if I can't get a Don Eagle, I still want to get it cut shorter so it is more controllable.

She wasn't happy with that idea, but thought it was preferable to my looking like a Mohawk.

The moral of the story is: If you want to do something your mother doesn't like, you should first offer an outrageous alternative. Anything you do after that seems tame by comparison.

So I got my flattop after all. I could now force any remaining curl out of my hair with wax that smelled like cinnamon.

Being a farm kid, anything you can do that makes you smell better is welcome.

TRYING TO DIET, DYING TO TRY IT

For many years I had been overweight. Women had not looked lustfully at me since—well—they've never really looked at me lustfully, but that's a whole other story.

Let me just say that my particular poundage piled on for the most part in the form of a protuberant pot belly. My belt buckle arrived on the scene well before the rest of me.

Potbellies is a trait that runs in my family. Even the men have them.

I suppose you can find an advantage in any physical disability or deformity if you look hard enough and make enough excuses about it. I'm sure the hard of hearing enjoy being able to turn off their hearing aids to shut out a screaming child. Extra tall people can reach high shelves.

Of course, there's a down side to both conditions. The hard of hearing can't fully enjoy music. The tall have to duck at doorways.

The chronically fat have their own set of problems. One of them is that we don't like to be called 'fat,' preferring instead to be referred to as heavy-set—or portly. Better yet, just call me by my name.

Formation of a pot belly may be Mother Nature's way of keeping a person farther from the dinner table to prevent it from growing even larger. There's that old saying: "The best exercise for losing weight is to push yourself away from the dinner table."

I personally do not prefer taking my meals in the dining room. I'm a casual diner. I think it may be rebelling against my mother's edict about not taking food into the living room, my personal favorite dining spot. My lounge chair is a place where a pot belly comes in handy as a kind of shelf for my plate. I could sit there with a book in one hand and a fork in the other, with my plate secure and in no danger of falling off its shelf.

But one day I concluded that a bay window was not only unattractive, it was also unhealthy. You hear stories about heart problems and diabetes linked to overweight. Just taking a walk was exhausting. My wife and I sometimes took walks. She likes to walk and talk, but I told her I could do one or the other—but not both.

I decided to get rid of the tummy. I applied my iron will to the project and over most of the next year I slimmed down by sixty pounds. I have nieces and nephews who don't weigh as much as I lost.

To be honest, women still didn't look at me lustfully. But I no longer opened a door by turning the knob and bumping it with my stomach.

The only disadvantage I can think of is that when I had lunch at my lounge chair, the plate kept sliding down onto my lap.

GOING TO THE MOVIES WITH GRANDMA

Saturdays were special in the 1940s. There was no school and it was the day I got my allowance. My 50-cents and I would get on a bus to the city to see a movie. The bus ride cost a dime. The movie ticket was a budget-busting 15-cents and a box of candy was a nickel. That left ten-cents for the bus ride home and one lonely dime for two comic books.

I would usually stop off at my grandmother's apartment in the city on the way to the show to say hello, maybe get a snack, and ogle the pretty nurses from Grandma's kitchen window as they went by on their way to the hospital next door.

"Where are you going, boy?" she would say.

"To the movies, Grandma," I'd say.

"Wait, I'll get my purse and go with you," she'd say.

"Uh . . ."

Now, when I said I was going to the movies, I meant I was going to the theater Grandma would not have been caught dead in. The grungy Rio Theater showed a western and mystery or comedy double feature, 24 color cartoons, a Three Stooges short subject, a Superman or Rocketman serial, and a live talent show on stage. We all got to holler and cheer and boo at what was on the screen, sit with our feet up on the orchestra pit railing, and be obnoxious where our parents couldn't see us.

But, what my grandma meant by "wait I'll get my purse and go with you" was, "we'll go to Loews Regent Theater." Instead of watching Lash Larue whip the bad guys into line or Red Ryder and Little Beaver thunder across the silver screen, we would be watching Howard Keel sing to Jane Powell. Or maybe it would be Fred Astaire dancing alternately with Ginger Rogers, Vera Ellen, Cyd Charisse, Ann Miller, or Mitzi Gaynor. And you couldn't holler and cheer or boo at what was on a classy screen like the one at Loews Regent Theater with its plush carpets and gilded decor. Certainly not with your grandma sitting right next to you. They didn't even have an orchestra pit railing and even if they had it would probably be covered with velvet and you wouldn't have been allowed to put your feet up on it.

But grandma paid for the tickets and the candy and I got to spend the time with her.

Many years later, long after Grandma had passed away, MGM came out with a video compilation of clips from their movies of the 40s and 50s.

Those Saturday mornings all came back to me in a warm wave as Howard and Mitzi and Cyd and Fred and all the rest sang and danced in glorious Technicolor.

But the best part of watching those videos was that for a couple of hours I got a chance to sit with my grandmother one more time.

STOP ME BEFORE I HURT MYSELF

I decided to build a small workshop. I gathered together all the tools and materials I thought it should take to do the job. Prior to that I had no experience at building anything bigger than a ham sandwich.

Well, a lack of experience, aptitude, and intelligence never stopped me before.

How hard could it be, right? It would be like Legos for grownups.

Not to be discouraged just because I have two left thumbs, I jumped headfirst into the project. My wife stood by in case I needed a second pair of hands—or an ambulance. The inept can use all the help they can get.

It was going to be a simple work area. I had bought a standing work bench at a yard sale. It was eight feet tall, four feet wide and two feet deep. It had upper and lower cabinets and drawers as well as a flat work counter. I built a rot-resistant redwood foundation to set it on a few paces from my back porch.

But I realized that if I expected to use it in rainy weather, my work space needed to be covered. So I built a roof that ran from the top of the workbench to two posts I put in the ground.

But even that didn't seem like much of a workshop and was certainly too small to store anything in. So I added a 10' x 10' foundation next to it with a plywood floor and built a small frame structure on it. It was walled in and even had a little window for extra light.

Still not satisfied, I added a 10' x 10' side rooflet to store my lawn tractor and shovels and rakes and other gardening items that I avoid using as much as possible.

Now I had, in effect, a shotgun shed where I kept adding as my needs and compulsions dictated.

In the years since then I have learned that a proper roof needs a slanted overhang so rain can drain away from it without getting the wood siding wet. I didn't know that, so the roof is without an overhang or a slant and the shed looks like something a gang of kids would build out of scrap lumber to use as their clubhouse. In fact, I put a sign on it, "No Gurls Aloud."

If I stand back and look at it, I wonder what I must have been thinking. But when I see that everything inside is dry, secure, and well preserved, I can't really complain. If I had it to do over again I would do a lot of things differently, of course. I've built other things since then and can now claim some basic competence, if not expertise, in that department.

So there it sits, all ugly and efficient. I've stopped apologizing for my earlier lack of knowledge. My little shed does just what I need it to do.

It just goes to show you, if you don't know you can't do something, you can sometimes do it.

THE DREADED EAR WORM

Have you ever gotten a song stuck in your head that just won't go away? You hear a song and then it stays with you for days—sometimes weeks. Those are called "ear worms."

In a possibly related condition; I've had tinnitus for more than 40 years. It is ringing in the ears that can come from a number of sources, including damage from loud noises and, according to hearing specialists, having taken too much aspirin.

The constant ringing drowns out a lot of sounds. That can be really inconvenient at times. Without hearing aids I can't hear my own footsteps as I walk. I have dropped objects and not been aware of it. I recently lost a set of keys and that has been an ongoing frustration.

I understand from psychologists that they often have patients come to them because the ringing in their ears is driving them crazy. It doesn't bother me to that extent. I have adjusted to the condition.

Not to say that I'm *not* crazy, but it's for other reasons.

I mention the tinnitus because I have a theory about its relationship to ear worms.

My theory goes thus: I believe a song that repeats itself endlessly is nature's way of placing a pleasant sound over the offending one, drowning out the ringing—giving the tinnitus sufferer a psychological break.

In my own case, when one song fades, a default tune often takes its place. It's a bouncy little ditty, whose title I can't identify—as opposed to the fading worm, which is always a familiar one.

A line in an old TV commercial went: "It's not nice to fool Mother Nature." Well, I have a trick I play on her. When I get really tired of a song on that maddening loop, I purposely find a recording of a different song and play it repeatedly until it replaces the tiresome one.

I've become my own deejay.

OH NO! NOT THAT DREAM AGAIN

Do you have a dream that keeps coming back? I think psychiatrists have a term for that:

Whacko.

No, seriously.

For many years I worked in radio stations, first as a deejay, later as a news reporter. My recurring dream always takes place in a radio studio. It is either nearly news time as a newscaster and I don't have any news copy written—or I'm a disc jockey and my record is running out without another one set up to run. In either case, I am not ready—and I am panicked because I am on the verge of facing the dreaded "dead air."

I can't pinpoint the exact source of this trauma, although that has actually happened several times. Nobody died, was injured, or got fired on any of those real occasions. Still, the image continues to visit me.

This has been going on for years. I have become almost comfortable with it. Having retired more than a dozen years ago it's kind of interesting to get inside a radio station now and then, even if it is a dream.

My friend Jerry is a psychologist. I have never sought his advice on how to deal with my recurring dream, but I once gave him some advice on how to handle one of his patients who was stuck in a troubling mindset. I suggested that he grab them by the collar, lift them off the floor, and scream into their face, "GET OVER IT!"

He said he appreciated my suggestion, but felt it would probably not be very effective.

THE WORST KIND OF PETS

It's nice to have pets. Some kinds of pets, at least. My wife and I have three cats and a small dog. The kind I have a problem with are pet *peeves*.

Most of my personal peeves involve language and the misuse of it. Now, I will admit to not knowing everything about everything and there are no doubt things I say and write incorrectly. We won't count those. We will only consider the incorrect usage and pronunciation of words, terms, and expressions by others—even those I personally learned about as recently as—say—an hour ago. Ever afterward I feel empowered and entitled to look down my nose at offenders.

Most of what we know about speech we learned outside of classrooms. When we were young we talked like our friends talked. We wanted to fit in, so it was monkey-see-monkey-do time. We mimicked those we admired—or feared—but who had not necessarily paid attention in English class and didn't know nothing about hardly nothing. They immersed themselves in double negatives and dangled the bejeezes out of participles.

We have held onto those habits for the rest of our lives, despite what our teachers tried to drill into us.

A member of my own family who shall go nameless—my sister, Diane—pronounces the state of Massachusetts, "Massa-TOO-sus." That's the way her childhood friends referred to the Bay State and that is the way she still does, well into her seventh decade.

I believe if I hear the word "literally" used incorrectly one more time, my head will *literally* explode. It is a word that the mis-users apparently believe adds weight to what they are saying. "He was *literally* blown away . . ." "He was *literally* hopping mad . . ."

Unless the guy was physically lifted off his feet by wind or jumping up and down while angry, he was not *literally* hopping mad or *literally* blown away.

I realize that language must evolve. If language did not move forward we would all still be grunting like cave persons.

Not to appoint myself the Language Police—but you have the right to remain silent . . .

CHICKEN CORN SOUP: A TRADITION

Every year, when the feed corn growing in area fields was at the eating stage, church women in my Perry County Pennsylvania home area would make chicken corn soup as a fundraiser. I don't know if they still do. If so, a bowl of it would probably cost more than the quarter it cost in the 1950s.

Whatever the price, it's worth it because it was heaven in a paper cup with a plastic spoon.

My personal recipe, which is a long-standing Perry County tradition, is very simple:

First you steal a chicken

Defeatherize and clean it, boil it down, debone it, discard the skin and bones. Cut the meat into smaller pieces. Save the water you boiled the chicken in.

Then you walk out to a farmer's field and pick some corn. My dad always said to "Leave the money on the fence." I would say, "What if there's no fence," and he'd say, "Now you have the idea, son."

Okay, moving on:

You cut the corn from the cobs and add it to the chicken and broth.

Now here's the good part:

In a bowl, you mix an egg and a pinch of water or melted butter in some flour and mix it around until you have a dry dough with tiny eggy-floury chunklets and you drop those—a few at a time—into the boiling soup. Those are called rivels (RIH-vuhls) and they add to the magic.

After it has boiled awhile, salt and pepper it to taste.

There you have it.

But I have to admit, the homemade version is nowhere near as good as those church ladies made.

Maybe it's because everything tastes better when someone else does the cooking.

NOBODY LIKES A COMPLAINER

You know how people say, "I don't like to complain, *but . . .?*" Well, complaining is not something I *like* to do. Not just because it doesn't do a bit of good to moan about this and that. No, I try to avoid complaining around other people because they don't want to hear it. They have their own problems and don't want to take on mine.

You want to kill a conversation, just start complaining about something—anything—and watch as people drift away from you. The more often a discouraging word is heard, the more cloudy the skies are all day.

Complaining takes many forms. Say you're at a four-way stop intersection and some clodhopper pulls out in front you when it's not his turn. You lay on your horn, make all kinds of specialty hand gestures, and scream nasty bits about the offender's maternal parentage.

Who do the other two drivers at the intersection get upset with? Not the aforementioned clodhopper who cut you off. They stare white-hot daggers at the guy making the fuss.

Nobody likes a complainer?

When people greet you with "Hi, how you doin'?" you are expected to say, "Great, how're you?" Start unloading woes on them and watch as their eyes glaze over and they remember meetings they're late for.

I am here to tell you that, while nobody wants to hear your beefs, it is injurious to one's health to keep it all bottled up. Something has got to give. An outlet must be found for the steam that is building, threatening to explode your head.

Mental health professionals are of no use at all. In fact, when they say, "and how do you feel about that?" you know they're not really listening and that just ticks me off that much more.

I can't even get it out of my system by yelling at my wife. She knows where the frying pans are and I have to sleep sometime.

OLD HABITS DIE HARD

Strange how we get locked into routines. For example: To make space for my paper shredder I moved my office wastebasket a few feet from where it has been for many years. Yet I still forget and toss scrap at the spot where the container used to be. I spend a lot of time picking stuff up off the floor.

About the same time as I retired, the battery in my wristwatch died. I didn't replace it. Why bother? I didn't have to be anywhere on time—or at all. Yet, not a day goes by in the dozen years since I stopped wearing it that I don't look at my bare wrist. If I really have to know what time it is, I can look at my cell phone. I don't even have to remember appointments anymore because my cell phone alarm can be set to remind me.

Another habit I can't seem to get rid of has to do with shifting gears on my pickup truck. I don't have to shift gears because the truck has an automatic transmission. It had been at least thirty years since I last drove a vehicle with a straight stick, yet I still occasionally come close to stepping where the clutch pedal would be if there were a clutch pedal, which there is not.

To make things worse, we recently bought a new Toyota that has—you guessed it—gears you have to shift the way the pioneers did.

It didn't take me very long to adapt to shifting gears. The real problem is that now when I get into my pickup truck I sometimes forget where I am and stomp down on a clutch pedal that isn't there.

Now here is a real puzzler that makes me think my brain may have retired around the same time as the rest of me did: When I was a new driver, a hundred years or so ago, I often took my little brother, Paul, with me. In those pre-seatbelt days he would sit next to me. When I pushed the brake, I would automatically put my arm up in front of him to keep him from falling forward.

As recently as two years ago I hit the brake on my truck and raised my arm as though I were protecting my brother.

Paul would have been seventy years old in October.

IGNORE GERMS AND THEY WILL GO AWAY

Maybe it's a "guy" thing in general, but I know it is a personal thing that I am not overly concerned about germs. Not bugged about bugs, you might say.

Oh, I do take precautions about some kind of germs; I wash my hands when returning from errands to try to eliminate the flu or the screamin' meemies one picks up in crowds at the grocery store or the post office or mingling with those little two-legged Petri dishes known as—children. They absorb every germ in the universe, share them generously with others, and rarely get anything worse than the sniffles themselves.

I am, however, a firm believer in the ten-second rule as applied to picking up a dropped food item and I am especially convinced we are far too fastidious when it comes to our coffee makers.

My wife regularly runs vinegar through her coffeemaker and scours the pot as though the Black Death is lurking within that particular appliance.

I, on the other hand, have used the same coffee cup since the last century, dumping out the previous day's leftovers and filling it with the new brew. The last time I cleaned my office coffee maker was when ants got into it. I can abide some germs, but I draw the line at ants.

My grandmother's theory of germ control—"heat purifies"—is good enough for me and she lived to be really old. Celebrity chef Julia Child was of the same school of handling dropped food: "Pick it up and pop it into the pot," she'd say.

I'm not saying that scum is particularly appetizing, but we don't have to get so worked up about it. Germs have feelings, too, you know.

I'm pretty firm in my sanitation theory as applied to dropped food, coffee makers, and cups.

I'm still working on the question of why women live longer than men.

GARDENING WITH A BLACK THUMB

I've heard that to become an expert at anything you have to practice it 10,000 hours. Ted Williams said it took him that long swinging at a baseball coming at him at 90-plus miles-per-hour to become the hitter he became. I'm sure it applies equally to basketball shots, golf swings and putts—just about every endeavor that requires us to lock an activity solidly in place.

The only area where I think that logic has failed on a personal level is my lack of competence at gardening—weeds aside. When it comes to growing weeds, I am in a class by myself.

After at least 10,000 hours of trying to grow flowers, trees, and vegetables, I have become an expert at killing them. If it were a felony I would probably be charged with flora-cide. I'm told that I have a black thumb. That is the opposite of a green thumb, which implies competence at making things grow. It has been suggested that I should probably buy my starter plants already dead to eliminate the middle step.

A friend of ours comes to visit about once a year. She can walk past a wilted plant and it jumps to attention. She can say hello to a philodendron and it explodes from the pot. I have watched her closely and can't figure how she works her magic.

I've read all the books and taken the suggestions about soil preparation, plant food, watering—every aspect of keeping things alive. I have been an attentive gardener. I even talk to plants. Please don't spread that around because half the people I know already think I'm nuts and the other half knows it for sure.

So you can imagine my surprise when I ripped a rosebush out of the ground at one place and jammed it into the soil at another, adding no nutrients and giving it only enough water to get it started. To my flabbergastment it has begun to sprout greenery instead of brownery. I cannot recall that ever happening before. Is it possible that I have reached a 10,000 hours failure level and have transitioned to success?

I have a theory. Instead of lovingly caring for a plant as I usually do, I took no special care and it is going just fine. Was disgraced former Vice President Spiro Agnew correct, that "benign neglect" is the way to go? He wasn't talking about plants, but it apparently applies.

It is very possible that I have been loving my plants to death?

THE PASSAGE OF TIME

People of a certain age hate being referred to as "People of a Certain Age." It is Political Correctness code for "Old."

Being of a certain age, I spend a lot of time these days thinking about time and the rapid passage of it. When I was in the army, I thought my hitch would never end. Every day was like a dog's days: seven days long. Those in bad marriages can tell you the same thing; time really drags.

Then you retire from that job that was never—ever—going to end and everything speeds up. You look back at past events and say, "I can't believe it has been15 years since I retired? Was it really three presidents and Donald Trump ago?"

Of course, when we're young we don't give much thought to time. We have no sense of it in the long term or that we will ever run out of it. Time-related thoughts in the young center on such events as the agonizingly slow approach of holiday breaks from school and the ooze of time until we're old enough to get a driver's license, our first car . . .

I have been alive more than 29,000 days. It was more than 10,000 days ago that I moved back to California. Trash pickup days flash by at warp speed. The lawn grows at a fearsome rate. I just mowed the back yard of my house yesterday—or was it last week—and it already needs mowed again.

If I'd had haircuts at the socially accepted two week intervals I would have had more than 2,000 of them. Of course, you would have to knock off a year or so at the beginning of life until I had my first haircut and my mother cried about it. Then you would have to subtract quite a few more at this end of life because I don't have enough hair left to waste a trip to—and the expense of—a barber. Clippers at home make short work of what little remains.

In fairness to Father Time and the Baby New Year, I should mention that not everything speeds up when you get older. It sometimes seems like that retirement check is never going to get here.

I'LL NEVER FORGET WHATZISNAME

As we get older, we sometimes have problems with our memory. Also, sometimes we have problems with our memory.

When I have trouble remembering something, I just ask my wife. I'll say, "You know, whatshisface, that guy—when we were at the—you know—the whatchacallit? Without fail Sherry comes up with the answer, no matter how vague the question.

I'm older than Sherry, so it stands to reason my memory would fail sooner than hers. I often say, "just wait until you're my age, you'll see . . ." Seven months later she is that age. But her memory just keeps chugging along.

Once I asked her if she could remember where we bought a teak desk with the burl inlay thirty-nine years ago and how much it cost. She not only remembered it, she pulled the receipt out of her file and showed it to me. The woman saves everything and never forgets anything. That makes it extra important that I don't offend her because she will remember that, too.

The downside of depending on someone else to remember things for you is that, more and more, you lose the natural ability to store things on your own that you will need later.

It works that way in this computer era, too. We get used to looking things up and, rather than digging down there in the far reaches of our own brains, we just tap out the question on a keyboard and there's the answer. Ever thereafter when the need arises we don't even try to rely on our own memories, we automatically ask Mr. PC or Mr. Mac.

When I remind myself of my lazy nature, I call upon my old reliable excuse: "That's just the way I am," and "I'm too old to change." It gets me out of a lot of stuff.

It's slothfulness, I know. It's a lot of effort to dig around among the neurons and get those synapses snapping. Besides, I don't want to overcrowd my brain with miscellany. There's only so much mental storage space and I've had a lot of years of cramming data in there. I figure I have just about reached capacity.

Until Sherry catches up with my memory lapses, she can be my Google.

WHAT OUR CARS SAY ABOUT US

Ever notice how many different makes, styles, and colors of vehicles there are on our American roads and highways? If you go to Spain, you will see an ocean of Siat (SEE-at) model cars in subdued colors and not much else. Siat is the Spanish version of the Fiat. You may occasionally see a BMW or even an upscale American car. However, if anything but a Siat breaks down in Spain it is going to be a long wait to get the part to fix it.

In this country we have lots of choices of makes, models, colors, and configurations. It's common to see a pickup truck with a noisy muffler and a body that is raised high above its oversized mud-grip tires. Most often the driver is male, in his mid-twenties to mid-thirties, has at least one tattoo, is a smoker, plays the radio loudly, and has rude and/or obscene bumper stickers on the back. Probably calls his wife "the old lady."

I remember when one of those loud, extra large pickup trucks roared up next to me at a traffic light. I craned my neck and looked up at the driver to see that it was a geeky little guy with glasses who must surely have been sitting on a kiddy seat so he could see out over the steering wheel. When he was in that truck he was as big as any man.

Crude skyscraper pickup truck drivers are not the only ones making a statement with their vehicles. We all do to an extent. Fire engine red and school bus yellow cars surely are saying something, although I'm not clear what that is. I could speculate that vivid red car drivers have a serious "Look at me" need and yellow car drivers may be advertising superior intellect.

There are a few Humvees still around, despite the high cost of gasoline. I interpret that as a driver wanting to project a military image whether or not he has ever served in the armed forces. All he needs is a macho military-like vehicle that gets six miles to the gallon.

He can be a hero and never leave his driveway.

Some vehicles are designed to dominate. They're the ones who come up dangerously close behind you on the freeway even though there is plenty of room to pass in another lane. They'll follow for a couple of miles, then whip out around you, nearly clip the front end of your car getting back in the lane they just left, and then drive at the same speed in front of you they were driving when they were behind you.

Then there are the cars that scream, "I'm rich!" They are the luxury car drivers who avoid the parking lot the rest of us have to use and park right in front of the supermarket to run inside for a few things. The privileged few. Their colors are rarely anything but black or grey, although they don't call them that. Rather they are "Parisian Ebony" or "Arctic Charcoal." I really shouldn't make too much of that since I once owned a Toyota Prius whose color was advertised as "Driftwood Pearl." We just called it "gold-ish" so people wouldn't think we were putting on airs.

My personal preference in a vehicle is one that starts every time, requires little maintenance, gets decent gas mileage, and transports me reliably and uneventfully from one place to another. I care little about what it looks like and only a little more about what it sounds like because I truly believe that my right to drive a noisy car ends at your ears.

Now, having said all of that I have to confess that at one time or another in my life I have been one of everybody I complain about now, in my geezerhood. I had cars with loud mufflers, loud radios, loud colors, and believed with all my heart that offending people was my God-given right as a red-blooded American teenager.

Now that I'm old and perfect I complain about people who are just like I used to be.

NO PLACE LIKE HOME

A huge percentage of the people who live in California come from somewhere else. That includes me. It is an automatic assumption that you are not from here.

It's not like that where I actually *do* come from. I think most people who live in Perry County, Pennsylvania started out there and are still there—or not far away. I seem to be an exception.

Careers sometimes send you to places you would not have chosen on your own. The weather is often a factor that drives people south. Itchy feet is a common cause among the young.

When people ask me where I'm from, even though I have lived in a lot of places and been all over the world, it's an easy answer; I claim a little green hunk of paradise among rolling Pennsylvania hills and sparkling streams. It has a rich history that goes back well before we were the United States of America—and has a population that appreciates it.

I'm sure many who still live there don't see my ancestral home as I do. The grass is always greener on the other side of the fence. I looked over that fence in 1958 and set off for what I thought were greener pastures. In fact, it turned out to be many years of bumpy roads and stormy skies.

It is true that times would not always have been rosy if I had stayed closer to my roots, but in all the other places I've lived, I never felt truly connected. If you are going to have troubles anyway, it is more comforting to suffer them among those you grew up with. They forgive you your shortcomings because they were standing right next to you when you acquired them.

Thomas Wolfe wrote, "You can't go home again." It's true. But not because where you came from has changed. It is because *you* have changed.

Still, there will always be enough of Home that stays with you to keep you warm when life gets cold.

THE AMERICAN DREAM

I don't know how you define the American Dream, but my dream is to have a hundred-acre ranch far from what we jokingly refer to as "civilization."

If we had that much land, I would draw an X on the property map. Where the lines intersected I would build my dream house.

We already have a small ranch. I used to call it a horse ranch, but we don't have horses anymore, so we're back to trying to justify calling it a ranch at all.

With a hundred acres we would be surrounded by a large amount of absolutely nothing. It would have to be fenced, of course. Without a fence, hunters tend to believe my property is their property during hunting season.

My wife says that's too much property to maintain. I say the acre or so with the house and outbuildings is all that will need maintained. The rest can just sit there and be a buffer zone.

Of course, we couldn't shed all of what civilization offers. I have to have U.S. Postal and UPS delivery services. An Internet connection is a must and at least a couple of bars showing on my cell phone. At my advancing age, nearby health care would be handy. Also, I don't want to have to drive too far for groceries or live beyond the point where my electrician, plumber, and appliance repair people would be willing to drive.

I know, I know. You're saying you want to get away from it all without getting away from all of it.

Hey, it's my American Dream and I'll dream whatever I like.

77

SHEDDING BAD HABITS

I quit smoking in 1964.

I quit drinking alcohol in 1988.

I quit chasing wild women in 1977. I never did catch any of the wild ones anyway.

It has been years since I was last kicked out of a restaurant for dancing on a table or got stopped for drunk driving.

I am no fun at all anymore.

There are certainly benefits to putting aside bad habits and wicked ways. For example: If I had followed the family tradition of continuing to smoke cigarettes, there is no doubt in my mind that I would be sitting here dead.

The roadways are much safer with one less drunk out there who doesn't really think he is impaired and who believes with all his heart that he is a better driver drunk than most people are sober.

As for the wild women; well, . . .

That is not to say that I no longer have any bad habits. There is no junk food item in our pantry that will not be attacked almost as soon as the groceries are packed away. And it is well known that I would get into a stranger's car for ice cream.

Plus, I am a sandwich guy to the extreme. Dagwood Bumstead and Hoagie Carmichael are my heroes. I need clamps to keep my two-story sandwiches from falling apart. I am such a sandwich devotee, I told my wife that when I die I want to be buried between two large slices of bread.

I could also do a better job of trimming down my To-Do list, but it grows even faster than the lawn I have been neglecting to mow. I'm already on page two of the list and I use a really small font.

There's no point in my making New Year's resolutions. Statistically those don't survive more than a few weeks after January 1st. Mine have never made it past the twelfth stroke of midnight.

Not to make excuses for myself, but I am not alone in putting things off until tomorrow which, by the way, never comes because tomorrow presents us with still another tomorrow and so on and so forth—and so fifth.

I could organize a procrastinators club, I suppose. But anyone who showed up at all for meetings would be at least a day late.

CONFESSIONS OF A GARAGE SALE JUNKIE

It's amazing how much "Stuff" a person can accumulate over the years, adding one item at a time. One day you look around your house and say to yourself, "we are in real danger of an avalanche."

If you are "of a certain age" (I hate that term because I *am* of a certain age), you may remember the "Fibber McGee and Molly" radio show of the 1940s. Fibber had a closet that was so crammed with "Stuff" that every time he opened the door, everything came thundering out of it. Our entire house is a lot like Fibber McGee's closet.

I am a certified (or is that "certifiable") garage sale junkie.

There, I said it.

There is no cure for an attraction to other people's "Stuff" and there are no organized support groups where people with a similar addiction can meet and tell their sad stories—and swap weekend sale site locations.

When we are driving along and spot a garage sale sign, my car's steering wheel actually vibrates—swear to God—and sometimes turns on its own and does not settle down until we are parked in front of the sale site.

It's not my fault, man.

I once had a two year record of never having missed a Saturday garage sale day. Perfect attendance at church would win me a medal, but there are no medals for perfect attendance at garage sales.

In northern California we have a lot of good weather, so the sale season is pretty much a year-round thing. *Neither* snow nor *rain nor* heat nor gloom of night shall keep me from my appointed rounds.

My wife, Sherry, routinely tells me as I'm about to hit the sale circuit, "If you buy something, you have to get rid of something to make room for it." Well, that's never gonna happen. I worked hard for those treasures. I spent more for gasoline than those things are worth, so there is an investment component here.

Okay, back to my story of too much "Stuff" which, by the way, is not a concept I necessarily subscribe to. Most people call extra rooms in their homes "guest bedrooms" or "dens." One of the extra rooms in our house is used as a pantry and for storage of a lot of the "Stuff" I have accumulated in my excursions.

I am certainly going to do something about that. One of these days.

My mantra is similar to that of someone addicted to drugs or alcohol. "I can quit anytime I want to."

And I will give it some serious thought, right after I check out half-price day at the local thrift store.

CHIP, THE WONDER DAWG

All I ever wanted in a dog was a big goofy animal that sat when you told him to sit and didn't chase chickens. I love dogs but, truthfully, we didn't want a dog at all because a house with three cats sharing space with two aging humans is already near capacity.

It started one Friday night. You know how, when it's dark outside and you think you see something running across your back yard? Black on black. Kind like of Mafia hitman's shirt and tie. Well, we didn't know it at the time, but that was our introduction to a little Jack Russell terrier.

We didn't see him in daylight until early the next evening, which was a Saturday. He had apparently escaped from somewhere. He had been running around for awhile and possibly mistreated in that time. He finally came to my wife. She brought him into the house, and put him in her bathroom temporarily to separate him from the kitty herd. It was late in the day, too late to take him to the county animal shelter. The shelter was closed Sunday.

Meanwhile, he was turned loose in the house and seemed to be enjoying the company of the cats and they his. He turned out to be a really friendly people dog. He climbed up on my lap, cuddled under my arm, looked up at me with big, brown, wet, pleading eyes, and by Monday morning there was no way he was going to the animal shelter.

We took him to the vet to see if there was any ID embedded in him. There was not. What he did have was a fractured jaw, some bruises—and cooties. We figured he had gotten into a disagreement with a trash truck or maybe got kicked by one of the equines we had at the time. We accommodated the fractured jaw by feeding him soft food. We couldn't tell if he'd had his shots, so we brought those up to date. We had an ID chip installed and named him "Chip." We also had him—ah—neutralized.

To make a long story even longer, hundreds of dollars later we had repaired and taken ownership of a Jack Russell terrier with more energy than is generated by all the solar panels in America.

Just imagine a team of Jack Russells hitched up to a sled. They'd be a shoo-in to win Alaska's Iditarod.

Chip occasionally gets super excited and races back and forth from one end of the house to the other. We call it "turboing" and we step aside for fear of getting bowled over by a 15-pound dynamo traveling at high speed.

Life in our household was changing dramatically.

Cats, as you may know, are relatively self-sustaining. They tend to go their own way pretty much, requiring only food, water, a clean litter box, and an occasional lap. Otherwise we lived in peaceful harmony, making few demands of each other.

A dog is different. A Jack Russell dog is *really* different. He requires at least two walks a day to run off some of that incredible energy and because we can't let him out on his own or he would be in the same dangerous situation we rescued him from.

Chip the Wonder Dawg, as I have taken to calling him, wrestles with Willow, the cat, who is the same size and weight as Chip. As far as we can tell, each is happy with the arrangement, neither fears the other, and nobody has gotten hurt.

The moral of this story is that a Jack Russell terrier is not a dog for older people.

But the only way you will get him away from me is with help from Seal Team Six.

ADVENTURES FOR MEN ONLY

For a few years, while recovering from a back injury that made it impossible for me to work in my profession as a radio news anchor, I worked for the local school district. One day I looked around Cubicle City and said to my friends, Jerry and Mike, "there sure are a lot of women in this place."

They looked around the big room and allowed as how I was right.

"We ought to get out of here and do stuff that women wouldn't even want to do," I said.

We were the only men in the entire department, not counting the big boss—and who would want to spend another day with that guy?

We three decided to start doing brazenly chauvinistic off-campus activities that excluded women. We would go to movies that had a lot of shooting and fights and loud explosions and car chases and minimally-clad actresses.

We would take day trips to places that forbade daintiness or anything painted pink, and maybe even say things you wouldn't say in front of your mother or others of refined sensibilities. We would spit and cuss and scratch and do guy stuff. We would exchange stories of our misspent youths that we would never even tell our doctor, priest, attorney, psychiatrist, or bartender—though they were sworn to secrecy.

My immediate boss heard about the proposed adventures. She said, "It sounds like fun, can I come?"

We were appalled at the idea that a woman wanted to take part in something specifically designed *sans la femme—what* Mike suggested we call "Man Town." I said, "We can't call it Man Town if there are women involved." She walked off in a snit.

Our test run involved a Saturday drive to Lake Tahoe where I lost my traditional twenty-dollar gambling limit to a hungry slot machine within mere minutes of our arrival. Then we drove around the area, taking in the awesome view of the lake and making manly comments about bikini-clad fauna on spring break.

On the way back home we stopped in the California gold country town of Placerville for lunch and more rowdy fun.

Man Town had turned out to be everything we imagined it would be.

Monday morning my boss came to me and said, "So, . . . how was your—Man Town? I thought there was a curl of the lip when she said the words.

"It was great," I said.

After a long pause, waiting for details and getting none, she said, "So, . . . what did you guys do?"

"We went to Tahoe and played the slots," I said.

"That's it?" she said. "Then what?"

"I *really* shouldn't tell you that."

Then I let her talk me into telling her.

"On the way back we stopped off at . . . 'Sweetie Pies.'"

She did a double take, then said, "What's that, a strip joint?"

"I promised the other guys I wouldn't tell."

I let that hang there for awhile before I finally told her it was a Placerville restaurant that specialized in pies.

That was fifteen years ago. All three of us are long retired now and we still get together at least once a month. We still take in the occasional movie, but more often we just have lunch somewhere and insult each other in good fun. One recent adventure series involved a quest for the world's best hamburger. The search has taken us all around much of northern California, laughing all the way.

I don't expect to ever find the ultimate burger. But that isn't really the object, is it?

PLAYING CHICKEN WITH A CHICKEN

Every morning I have two visitors at the door to my little backyard office.

They are Rhode Island Red roosters who have come for breakfast, which consists of about a quarter slice of bread each and a handful of scratch feed.

One is a shy guy who never gets closer to me than a few yards. The other I have named "Big Red." I call him Big Red because he's, . . well, . . . big . . . and red. He has more personality than George Clooney and I have come to consider him part of our family.

I know you're not supposed to have favorites among your children, but I have become very attached to the boy. He stands at my feet and takes the bread right out of my fingers. Sometimes, in his exuberance, he almost takes the finger. I don't hold it against him. He probably doesn't get any more food than he finds on the ground.

Breakfast, after all, is the most important meal of the day.

Red and his pal are not really ours. They are the property of the handyman at the cemetery next door to our little ranch. For us it's like having chickens without having chickens.

We are hoping that Red is considered a pet by his legal owner rather than as a future dinner because I like seeing the big galoot far more on my office porch than I ever could on a platter. Frankly, I think he is too old and tough for the menu, but the cemetery handyman is also old and tough, so who knows?

The prevailing thought about roosters is that they crow at dawn. Indeed they do. They also crow at midnight, 3:12 a.m., noon, 4:37 p.m. and any other time that pleases them. Maybe I should have named him Pavarotti because when he belts out his song it could be heard all the way to the back row of the opera house—or, in this case—rattle our bedroom windows.

His cock-a-doodle-doo interrupt's my wife's sleep. Sherry wakes up if one of our cats sighs. Not me. I have been known to sleep through gunfire, explosions, howling coyotes, and cargo planes that fly low over our house.

Taking Chip the Wonder Dawg for a walk is also a challenge. Before Chip and I go out for his twice-daily walks I have to scan the area for renegade chickens. Big Red and Chip don't like each other.

Since they are about the same size, it's a tossup as to who would eat whom if it came right down to it.

ANNUAL VISITORS, HONORED GUESTS

Every year, anywhere from the first week of January to the first week in March, we are honored by a visit from a pair of Canada geese. They make their nest on an island in a pond adjacent to our property. The hitch is that they nest on the island only if it is not a drought year and if the water level has come up sufficiently. Otherwise it is just a large clump of dirt in the middle of a huge hole in the ground.

Coyotes like to make a meal out of geese, so it is critical that there is a moat around their birthing grounds. We never know whether there will be enough rain to fill the hole. The Canadas send scouts ahead to make sure it is safe to camp here for the spring and summer. We got lucky this year. The pond is a pond and the geese have arrived.

We think the arrivals are a pair from previous years because they didn't fly away when I approached them close to our back yard. I tossed some cracked corn for them, but they didn't seem especially interested. That will change.

As we have learned over the years, there is a regular routine to building trust. Even though these geese probably have some memory of us buried deep in the back of their little bird brains, they are still cautious at the beginning. As time passes, they come closer and enjoy the food we provide.

We will see both of them floating on the pond for several weeks. Then, we will only see the male. That means Mother Goose is setting the eggs she has added to the nest one at a time in those weeks that we saw both of them.

The countdown begins.

It takes 21 days to hatch a goose egg. So, three weeks from the day Mom disappears—give or take a couple of days—we can expect to see little fuzz-balls floating on the pond. I say give or take a couple of days because the female has to put the kids through basic training. First she has to waterproof them so they won't sink. She does that by applying goose oil to their fluffy little bottoms. That done, it's off to swimming lessons.

I'm sure they go through Survival 101, which consists of Mom telling them that if some critter approaches that is larger than they are—and, at this point, that's just about everything—they should skadaddle as fast as their tiny webbed feet can propel them.

As Tarzan must certainly have said to Jane, "It's a jungle out there."

As the weeks go by they will grow larger and larger and come closer and closer to us for their twice-daily rations. By July they will be milling right around our feet, with Dad hissing at us. He knows we're not going to hurt his babies, but part of the Dad code requires that he hiss a warning, just in case.

Then, one day we will hear honking. It will mean Pop Goose and the little ones—that are no longer little—are in flight training to prepare them to fly away and join the larger flock and get ready to migrate.

No more than two days later, they are gone without a goodbye or a honk of thanks.

It is always a sad day and the best we can do is hope they will come back to us next year.

VOTE THE RASCALS OUT

Discontent with the federal government is at a level not seen since the Nixon administration four decades ago.

What's to be done about it?

Well, we could clean house all around; vote the whole bunch of them out of office. But there is plenty of motivation for those officeholders to stay on the job. Where else could they get health care coverage and retirement plans like that? Not to mention the other perks of office: trips to exotic places to allegedly study this and that. They don't like to call those trips "junkets" because that sounds too much like unnecessary luxury freebies at taxpayer expense.

It can cost millions of dollars to win a U.S. Senate or House of Representatives seat that pays $174,000 a year plus health care and retirement benefits far greater than the average American will ever enjoy. And they are fully vested after just a few years on the job. A Senator who has served a single six-year term can retire with a $139,200 lifetime monthly pension check. Likewise a Representative who serves three two-year terms.

Ask any voting American—and many who don't vote but complain about the what is going on in Washington—what should be the first step toward getting a Congress that actually works in the taxpayer's interests and you will get the same answer: "vote the rascals out."

However, they don't mean *their* rascals, they mean *your* rascals. When election time comes around they routinely vote for the incumbent in their district. "It's the Senator in Montana who should be kicked out," says the voter in Missouri. "It's the Congressman in Pennsylvania who should be shown the door," says the voter from Utah. The power of the incumbency is staggering. In part it is because the person who already holds that office has all manner of promotional opportunities at his and her disposal: free U.S. Mail services, appearances before the media to sing their own praises. The incumbent's challenger has no such platform or the name and face recognition that goes with it.

The number of Senators and Representatives in Congress whose personal fortunes grew while in office is unbelievable. More than a few Congress members who were broke when they took office have retired as millionaires.

Keep in mind that they make the laws that give them those special benefits and opportunities.

I once knew a state senator—I won't mention the state—who owned a new car dealership. He didn't take cash under the table. That would have been illegal. But he did sell a lot of cars to CEOs of companies maneuvering for his support the next time a vote came up that favored that company.

Here is another myth that needs to be debunked. Lawmakers seldom write the laws and industry regulations they sponsor. Those are frequently written by lobbyists who represent special interests. They are full of loopholes that, in effect, mean there is no regulation at all. When confronted with a violation, the company representatives can simply say, "We followed the law." What they don't say is that they wrote that law.

And here is another sad fact: Except for how it affects their chances for reelection and keeping them out of prison, these lawmaking violators of the public trust don't really care what you think about it. They will continue to do whatever benefits them.

Next election, vote for the opposing candidate so the person you voted out of office can join a lobbying firm and make some real money.

A CONSPIRACY TO KEEP US POOR

I suppose everyone hopes that one day their ship might come in so they can drop out of the Rat Race and live a life of ease. Well, my ship hasn't come in yet, but occasionally a rowboat shows up at my virtual dock.

The problem with that is that when there is that rare occurrence, someone—or circumstances—comes along to relieve me of the responsibility of any windfall.

I'm sure it happens to everyone to some degree; you get five bucks ahead and that very day there will be a bill in the mail for $5.27. You hold a garage sale, make a tidy $50.00 and the doorbell rings to announce the arrival of a tax bill, sewer assessment notice, or, or, or—.

It's enough to make a person think there is an organized conspiracy in effect to keep you in that financial rut.

Over the years I have developed a theory: A government agency is working hand-in-hand with private enterprise. They send guys around your neighborhood to keep track on any financial progress you might make.

If you look outside your home right now, across the street, by a lamp post or behind a tree, an agent is probably there—clipboard in hand—writing down bits and pieces of information about you. As each scrap of data come in about the few dollars you manage to accumulate, he reports to someone who can relieve you of it—plus ten to twenty-percent more.

Let me give you just one example of how I know it's true.

After a glorious two week vacation in Spain I was at the Madrid airport waiting to board my plane for home. Boxes of souvenirs were piled high on the luggage scale.

After buying up half of Spain, I found I still had $60 remaining in my wallet.

"That will be $54.80," said the airline clerk.

"For what?" I said.

"It's the overweight fee," she said.

I reluctantly paid the fee and made my way to my plane with just $5.20 in my jeans. Not even enough for a taxi home from the airport in the U.S..

I had to call a friend to bum a ride.

When I went to the post office the next day to pick up my vacation mail there was a box rent bill for $6.50.

As I left the post office I could swear I saw a man duck out of sight around a corner. I think he was carrying a clipboard.

LET'S NOT PUNISH THE INNOCENT

I suppose it is human nature to be wary of an individual who has offended, injured, disrespected, or committed a crime against us. It is natural to be reluctant to allow that person to ever get close to us again or to enjoy a position of trust.

But is it right to distrust an entire race, religion, occupational group, or political body because of the actions of a few? That kind of thinking got Japanese-Americans imprisoned during WWII. They looked like the enemy, so they were treated like the enemy and locked up—just in case.

There is a theory making the rounds these days that, since a group of terrorists that uses Islam as its umbrella organization is forcing a malignant version of Islam on the world, then all followers of Islam must also be bad and all Muslims should be imprisoned or booted out of America and no more allowed in—just in case.

There were good Germans during World War II who fought against the Nazis and supported the Jews that were so hated by Adolph Hitler and his evil band of followers. There are Muslims who resent that their religion has been hijacked by a band of thugs who believe that those who do not worship as they do should be destroyed.

As difficult as it might be to believe, there are more good members than bad ones in our gridlocked Congress. Outright thieves are in the minority. The other kind are in the news, hungry for your attention, their aspirations for re-election, and for higher office and feathering their own nests.

There are a lot of good cops out there who are working to make their cities and towns safe. It is wrong to target all police because of a few rogues that make the news.

Let's not punish the honorable and the innocent while punishing the guilty.

Let's not treat everyone like the worst one.

95

LET'S TRASH WHAT DIVIDES US

Proof of how people pull together in a crisis happens all around us nearly every week. When a madman killed 49 people in an Orlando club, the entire community pulled together. We all remember Boston after the marathon bombing. Strangers came to the rescue of the injured. It happens in war, too. Soldiers faced with death daily rely on each other as they never had as civilians. When Paradise, California was destroyed by fire, leaving thousands homeless, the world swooped in to give aid.

Why then, can't we find that kind of reliance on each other in everyday life?

The answer may be that we are too comfortable. Nothing in the physical sense is threatening us in an average day.

Maybe what the world needs is a great tragedy to bring us all together. Sad, isn't it, that the only way we give of ourselves is in an emergency that requires us to be reliable so that we can rely on others for our own protection.

There are people out there right now who could benefit from what we know and what we can do that they do not have the skills, knowledge, or resources to do for themselves.

I'd like to see a world-wide outreach movement; people doing good, helping others just because it's the right thing to do, not just for self-preservation.

And let's do it before the pandemic, the terrorist attack, the asteroid strike, the famine, the nuclear holocaust, the economic collapse.

If you understand that you will have to do it then, you need to understand that you have to do it now.

A STAR WAS BORN

It was around Halloween 1976. My pal Bridget Sienna and I went to a dinner party in Hollywood. Bridget is an actress ("Rain Man," "The Groundlings," "Seinfeld").

My friend, actor Virgil Frye ("Easy Rider," "Colors") and his wife Sondra Peluce, were the hosts of the get-together. Sondra is a caterer who provides meals on movie locations. Their apartment was filled with the aroma of the ducks Sondra was roasting.

Guests included actress Piper Laurie, whose horror movie, "Carrie," was playing at the time. Several other show biz people were scattered around the living room; familiar faces whose names may be on the tip of your tongue, but you can't quite remember. Mike Pataki was one. He was in "Rocky V" and a lot of other films. Billy Green Bush was another. He played Vernon Presley, Elvis's dad, in the TV movie, "Elvis and Me" and Robert Blake's biker buddy in "Electra Glide in Blue."

Dinner was running late because Virgil kept opening the oven to see if the duck was done yet. That delayed the meal further because the heat kept escaping.

Marijuana messes up a person's sense of time. In his weed fog, Virgil apparently figured 20 minutes should be enough.

While we were waiting, Virgil said, "do you want to see the baby?"

We did.

So we went into the bedroom to have a look at their two-month-old girl who somehow managed to sleep through all the clatter in the next room.

The little one was only about a foot-and-a-half long and looked like every two-month-old baby you have ever seen—all pink and wrinkly. Fingers about the diameter of a spaghetti noodle.

I hadn't had much experience with babies. None of my other friends had children of any size. This was a novelty for me. On those rare occasions when I do encounter one that tiny it always blows me away that we could possibly have all started out like that.

I felt very old this week when I read on the newspaper's celebrity birthday list that it was that little baby's 42nd birthday.

The next time I saw her again was in 1984 when Soleil Moon Frye played Punky Brewster on TV.

LOVE ANIMALS, DON'T EAT THEM

For a long time my wife, Sherry, and I have been considering adopting the vegetarian lifestyle. In part because it is probably healthier. But even more than that it is because we love animals and feel that we should not be eating them.

We have concluded that we are guilty of murder by proxy. That is, we have hired someone to do what we don't have the courage to do ourselves.

A nice young couple that travels around the country full time in their RV is an example of the value of avoiding meat. Olivia (vegan) and Kyle (99% vegetarian) Brady have a YouTube site at "drivin' and vibin'." They are living, rosy-cheeked proof of the health benefits.

My Facebook friend Beth, herself a vegetarian, shared a YouTube video of a man who adopted a turkey to keep the bird from ending up on someone's dinner table. The turkey apparently realized that his life had been saved and now gives his adoptive human regular hugs.

I think that was the final (turkey in the) straw that has pushed us over the edge toward vegetarianism. At least enough to give it a try.

It would be impossible for me to go entirely vegan and give up eggs, butter, and cheese. I think I would also reserve some seafood some of the time. I'm not sure what you would call that category. "Hypocrite" might describe it. After all, those are lives, too.

I know I would miss my bacon. We have a refrigerator and freezer full of meat right now, so Sherry and I have decided on a test run. We will stop buying all meat products immediately and each Wednesday and Saturday we will eliminate meat from our diet on those days. The goal would be to see whether we could sustain that diet over the long term—at the same time exhausting our meat stock.

Critics of vegetarianism argue that the human body needs meat or else some vital nutrients will be lacking from the diet. Vitamin supplements are needed for a meatless diet.

Practitioners of the non-meat lifestyle argue that horses and cattle are on a strict vegan diet and seem to do very well.

Whatever your position on the concept, lives are undeniably at stake and I believe all lives have value.

Thanksgiving and Christmas would be a whole lot different around here.

Maybe the next time I see a turkey I'll get a hug.

OFFICIAL OLD AGE INDICATORS

Remember when we used to call the newspaper comics "The Funny Papers?" It seems to me that fewer and fewer of the strips are actually funny anymore.

I supposed it's another sign of old age. It started with, "Whatever happened to *real* music," and "Back in my day. . ." Then cops, firefighters and college professors started to look like kids. Those were always the primary indicators that one has officially said goodbye to his and her youth.

Having been on the personal downhill slide for several years now, I have added to the decrepitude indicators: Comic strips I don't bother to read anymore.

When you have to decode or translate a comic rather than read through it smoothly to get to the punchline, it has lost all interest for me. Especially if there is no punchline. Some are so bogged down with dialog that by the time you get through it, it is has lost any possibility of a laugh.

Since most American newspapers have slimmed down their comics pages or substituted those that actually are funny with those that charge cheaper royalties, there aren't that many left that make it worth even opening the newspaper to the so-called "comics" section anymore.

I can understand that newspapers are in financial trouble. The Internet, coupled with increasing nationwide apathy, is putting a huge dent in newspaper circulation. Publishers are forced to cut corners everywhere they can.

I always regarded the comics as holy territory; the "third rail" of cost cutting areas. Like Social Security was to the elderly, although Congress has pretty much looted even that sacred ground.

Of the 35 comics that still appear in my daily newspaper, I continue to read 18 if them. Just this week I eliminated two more and there are seven others on the cusp.

I really want to support newspapers. I truly believe they are the only thing in these troubling times in Washington, DC that stand between Democracy and disaster.

Nothing as frivolous as my demanding that the funny papers be funny will stop me from continuing my subscription.

But these days more than ever we really could use some laughs.

CAT OWNER, AN OXYMORON

Nobody owns a cat. Let's get that notion out of the way right from the start.

My wife, Sherry, and I are owned by two cats. That is down from the twenty or so we have had over the past 40 years. The second of the current two was an outdoor volunteer. Rocky was pretty beat up and undernourished when Sherry considered bringing him indoors where it's safe from marauding critters that are bigger, faster, and meaner than he is.

Transitioning a career outdoor cat to the indoors is a bigger challenge than one might imagine. He had spent a large portion of his life as a gentleman of the road; a hobo, if you will; free as the breezes to do as he pleases.

But wait, there's more.

Before he came indoors you could set your watch by the time Rocky showed up at the back door of our house for his morning meal. That's why one morning when he wasn't there, we pretty much assumed that some night creature got him.

But on the third day he arose from the dread and there he was at the back porch, ready for breakfast. No explanation. Can't imagine where he had been for that all that time.

All was well until a month or so later when Rocky again did not make morning mess call. My mood was blue, but not the deep purple funk like the first time he didn't show up because there was the hope that he was okay—as he had been before.

But by the fourth day Rocky still had not appeared and we assumed the worst.

I was going about my ranch duties as usual when I heard what sounded like Rocky's voice. I followed the sound to the base of a 50-foot-tall cottonwood tree, but I couldn't pinpoint the exact location. I called Sherry on my cell phone and she joined me in the search.

"There he is," she said, pointing up in the tree.

Rocky was hanging onto a limb about 30 feet above us, beyond the reach of my 20-foot extension ladder. I went to a rental store and rented a 30-foot ladder. Even that wasn't enough because about the time I got to where Rocky was perched, he moved to an even higher limb.

"Why don't you call the fire department?" Sherry said.

"They're not going to want to come out to rescue a cat," I said. What a cliché.

Anyway, I drove to the nearest fire station where I met three young firefighters. I told them I felt like an idiot for even mentioning this and I would totally understand if they also agreed that I was an idiot—which most people do without my permission—and told them my story.

Not only did they agree, the whole crew got excited at the idea.

To make a long story just a little longer, the firefighters did not climb the tree, they squirted a thin stream of water above Rocky. He hates water more than he hates being 30-feet up a tree, so he jumped and clawed and hung on and finally made it to the ground—safe and sound.

Rocky is an indoor cat now. He is not without people skills. He rewards us for feeding him twice a day by allowing himself to be petted.

And did I mention he also gets free housing with a heating pad for winter and a cool, spot next to the air conditioner in the summer? His full-coverage health care plan rivals that of members of Congress. And, like Congress members, it doesn't cost him a dime.

THAT FIRST IMPRESSION

We once had 12 cats at the same time. Our herd is down to two now. We have lost many of our feline family members over the years.

Back in those cat-saturated days we bought all of our pet food once a month. It was quite a pile of cans there on the pet store checkout counter.

Almost without fail, the clerk or another customer standing nearby would say, "do you have a lot of cats?"

I would say, "No, just one very large one," and indicate a size of a jungle animal.

Ask a dumb question, get an impertinent answer.

I guess for some people, the obvious is not always obvious.

Or maybe they're just being friendly.

I have a friend who starts up conversations with whoever is standing closest to him. In all the years I have observed Mike reaching out to strangers, no one has ever seemed to be offended or put off by his boldness.

If I were to do the same thing, parents would draw back and hustle their children behind them for protection. Old ladies would reach into their purses for pepper spray. Young women would call out in a quivering voice for a security officer.

I don't get it. Does my friend look unthreatening and I look like the devil personified?

Mike makes a lot of friends. I make the FBI's ten most wanted.

We each have the same goal; to be friendly and maybe expand our world a little.

I have known for many years that I don't always make a good first impression. A guy who has since become one of my best friends once said to me, "when we first met I didn't like you at all." At the time, I couldn't imagine why, my heart being pure and all that. I guess some people just have to grow on you.

I admire my friend Mike's outgoing ways and I have since tried to be more sociable. I'm getting better at it. Fewer people back away from me in fear these days.

Progress is welcome in whatever form it takes.

A MECHANICAL GENIUS

I once worked with an extraordinary man named Jiggs. He was in charge of the print shop at the weekly newspaper in Pennsylvania where I was an editor for a couple of years.

Jiggs could fix anything. He'd take a look at the problem, figure out how it worked—or stopped working—and, before you could say Supercalifragilisticexpialidocious, he'd have it diagnosed and back in service. Since he was often working with century-old printing equipment, parts were rarely available and he would have to improvise.

"If all the paper clips I've used to fix things were to disappear," he said, "this whole place would collapse."

Jiggs passed away a few years ago and I have often wondered how his fixit-skills would survive in this age of plastic. Even Gorilla Glue can't do much for a material that deteriorates in the hot summer sunshine.

We recently bought a wireless weather station. It is mounted high on a pole in our back yard. It transmits information to a screen in the kitchen of our house about the wind speed and direction, the temperature, humidity, barometric pressure, phases of the moon, and rainfall amount. It even shows when rain is forecast. It is a truly amazing instrument. But it is made of—you guessed it— *plastic*. Being a weather device, it is out in—you guessed it again—the *weather*. Extreme climate conditions and PVC do not get along well, so it's anyone's guess as to how long it will last.

I just know that Jiggs is out there somewhere, looking down at a world largely made of plastic.

I wonder if they have paper clips in Heaven.

SOPHISTICATE VRS CLODHOPPER

Do you want to look sophisticated? Do you want people to think you're really hep? Do you want to appear as though you are cookin' with gas?

Okay, first of all don't use words like "hep" and phrases like "cookin' with gas." Nobody has said those since the 1940s.

What is it about some people that they hold onto the phrases of their day—long after their day?

I guess some are big fans of the passé.

"Radical" was worn out by the end of the 90s but I still hear it. I don't remember when "super" passed away, but it's still out there for those who have not "gotten the memo."

See? Now they have me doing it.

I once worked with a guy in the 1970s who, when someone said something interesting, he would say. "swingin'." That went out of fashion in the 1950s, along with "ginchy" and blue suede shoes.

"Cool" seems to have survived the ages, while "hot" has not. "Cool" jumped the acceptability barrier and continues as a symbol of approval.

Hard to say why some catchwords and phrases live on while others fall out of wide usage.

A woman I worked with did everything imaginable to appear chic, worldly, and way out there on the front lines of really smart stuff. However, her efforts were so clumsy that she came off looking like a hick.

She would use what she apparently believed were the current catch phrases, "Don't go there," and "I didn't see that coming," not realizing that they had long since been relegated to the conversational slag heap.

She apparently never heard the groans coming from others in meetings when she would throw in words like "Paradigm," "Algorithms," and "Modalities."

I guess she figured her bosses would think she was really hep.

TERROR ON ORE BANK HILL

My first car was a 1931 Model A Ford sedan. I don't think Ford called it a sedan. Probably some snooty name like "touring car."

It cost $50.00 and took me all summer working at a gas station in my hometown to pay for it.

I recently paid $75.00 just to fill up the gas tank on my Chevy pickup truck. For that kind of money I could have bought one-and-a-half Model A Fords. Unfortunately, it's not 1953 anymore and if you could find one in the same condition today it would cost many thousands of dollars.

I loved that car. But, of course, everyone loves his first car. Having a four-wheeled escape pod meant there was now a whole reachable world out there to explore. Prior to that, I couldn't get any farther away from home than my bicycle would take me.

As kindly as I felt toward that car, it was also the cause of one of the most terrifying experiences of my life.

I was driving over Ore Bank Hill, on the curviest road in the county. Once you reached the top, it was a steep downhill run for several miles, with nasty switch-backs and curves not banked to accommodate speeding vehicles and centrifugal force.

As I chugged to the top of the hill and started down the other side, I came to the first curve. I was picking up more speed than I was comfortable with, so I slammed on the brake. Young people do that a lot. Nothing subtle about most anything they do. A gentle pressing of the brake is not in a teen's playbook.

Well, the Model A had a rod that connected the foot pedal to the mechanical braking system under the car. The problem was, the rod was made of cast iron. Cast iron does not handle slamming very well and it snapped, leaving me in near free-fall. Those old cars had very little compression to help hold the speed down and it was impossible to down-shift in those pre-synchromesh transmission days.

So there I was, on the scariest road imaginable, careening downhill in a top-heavy vehicle with no brakes. I was seventeen years old and certain I would never see eighteen, whipping this way and that, wrestling the non-power steering wheel, skinny 21-inch tires squealing at every curve, picking up speed for several hair-raising miles.

Finally, I got to the bottom of the hill and was able to coast to a stop.

Thinking back to that experience I wonder once more how I managed to survive my youth.

Anyone who doesn't believe in God has never ridden a Model A Ford with no brakes down Ore Bank Hill.

WHINE WITH DINNER

Friends we used to hang out with in Los Angeles—well, *she* was the friend, her husband was a jackass—and I say that with apologies to donkeys everywhere.

It was one of those love-her-hate-him relationships where you have a really great friend, but have to take her pretentious jerk of a mate in the deal.

Anyway, among other irritating quirks, this guy was an art, theater, book, and wine snob.

Sometimes we would go to dinner with them. When the wine steward came to the table with a bottle, our snob would take over. The steward would hand him a cork, which our guy would sniff.

You ask me, if you smelled one cork, you pretty much smelled them all.

Then he would examine the label, to learn what year it was bottled and who did the bottling. He would nod nearly imperceptibly, cradle the wine glass in his hand—wrist bent appropriately—accept a small splash, swirl it around in the glass, sniff it—eyes closed, lips pursed—take a small taste and do one of those little inhaling slurpy things that sound a lot like when you let air out of a tire.

Then he would say something like, "Robust, but not aggressive," and "it has a prominent nose," both of which sounded more like a description of a heavy-set girl I used to date.

Then, appearing something short of satisfied, he would pronounce the wine acceptable and permit it to be served all around.

And the guy wasn't even the one buying the wine.

I don't drink anymore, but when I did I had my own little ceremony.

The wine guy would bring a bottle. I would check to make sure there were pictures of grapes on the label. I couldn't have cared less when it was bottled. The day before yesterday would be just fine with me.

I didn't bother to smell the cork. I was always amazed that there even *was* a cork and not a screw-top.

Then I'd tell the guy to start pouring and keep it coming.

I'd like to believe I have more class than our ex-jackass, but I proudly admit to being a Neanderthal who bought wine by the jug.

THE GOSPEL ACCORDING TO THE INTERNET

According to the Internet, I have been doing just about everything all wrong my entire life.

One morning MSN had an article that assured me that I have not been cooking steaks properly to get maximum flavor out of them.

Imagine my surprise when I learned that I had been peeling bananas all wrong; I should be opening them from the stubby end, they said, not the stem end.

I have always cooked pasta in salt water and added a dash of olive oil to the pot. That is supposed to keep the noodles from sticking together. NO, says the Internet! It's a waste of olive oil and you have been doing it WRONG.

The daily deluge of things I am not doing correctly has me wondering whether I might be doing everything else all wrong, too. My self esteem has been eroded. I have lost all confidence that I have any skills at all because the Internet keeps telling me I have been on the wrong side of right my entire life.

You can't stay that stuff on an Internet if it isn't true.

I went into the kitchen yesterday to make a sandwich. I was hesitant because now I'm wondering if I am making and consuming sandwiches all wrong. In the past I have always bitten into one with the mustard or mayonnaise on the upper-most slice of bread. But wait! Should I have put it on the lower-most slice? I am so confused. The Internet hasn't said anything about that, but now I'm afraid I have maybe been eating my sandwiches upside-down all these years and it has me a nervous wreck.

I always put both socks on at the same time and then the shoes. Is it possible I should be putting on a sock and a shoe and then the other sock and the other shoe? The Internet isn't clear about that and I wonder if that means that maybe I've been doing it okay. I have my doubts, though, since I've been cooking steaks, skinning bananas, and boiling pasta all wrong this whole time.

It's a wonder anyone who uses the Internet has a shred of self-confidence left.

I've tried to ignore those articles, but the headlines are always prominently displayed in bold letters, practically screaming at me that studies have been done by really smart people—probably scientists—that prove that I have been doing lots of things wrong. Those articles stick out so much that you almost can't help clicking on them.

Do you think I've maybe been a victim of fake news? There's supposed to be a lot of that out there. But who's to know which is fake and which is the real deal. I sure don't know because my self-confidence is in shambles.

After all, I'm a guy who apparently doesn't know one end of a banana from the other.

DISORDER ON THE COURSE

There are all types of mental disorders: bipolar, depression, eating, obsessive-compulsive, anxiety and panic, post traumatic stress, psychosis . . .

However, there is one serious mental illness that no seems to recognize as such. This particular affliction is sweeping the country and there is neither a known cure nor a medication to control it.

It's called Golf.

I have a friend who travels with his three brothers every winter from New York to Myrtle Beach, South Carolina, a city with more than 100 golf courses. That alone suggests there is something very creepy going on in that town.

The brothers usually spend three days knocking a little white ball all around vast manicured fields at great expense.

Imagine all the starving children in Boston, Chicago, New York, and Los Angeles those green fees could feed. And that doesn't even count the cost of the hotel, meals, and a frightening amount of booze.

Any normal player—I hesitate to say "Normal Golfer" because that is clearly an oxymoron—would lay off the game for the winter. Not so my friend and his brothers. Those guys have played—I'm not making this up—in the *snow*. They use a fluorescent orange ball and slog around the course in the actual snow. How they find the hole is a mystery to me. If that isn't certifiable I don't know what qualifies.

Who, with all their mental faculties, would purposely walk several miles, frustrate himself to the outer limits of profanity and spiked blood pressure to do such a thing?

I suspect the mindset may not be restricted to golf. There are people who actually ride on what we used to call roller coasters that are now called something with the name "Monster," "Killer" "Tornado," "Lightning," or "Thunder" in them, suggesting there is a measure of insanity involved.

Having said all that, I suppose if a person earns the money and wants to pay a couple of bucks to get on such a ride—which is upside-down for much of the trip—and then toss their cookies right after that, I guess it's their business.

I SEE DEAD PEOPLE

I watch just one TV show every week. That is, I watch one TV show on the TV. I get up early to watch "CBS Sunday Morning." Other than that, I don't even need a television set.

Now, my computer and iPhone are other matters. I subscribe to Amazon Prime and Netflix and I watch ghosts of television series and movies past. As actor Haley Joel Osment said in the film, "The Sixth Sense," "I see dead people." That's right, a lot of the actors on the old shows I watch are no longer with us. It's weird seeing the dead walking, talking, shooting, fighting, chasing crooks in cars, dead guys making out with babes who are probably just as freaked out these days as I am that they're kissing a dead guy.

Nothing to be done about it. That's the way it is in real life and in the show biz world; here today, canceled tomorrow.

When we see the rich and famous all glammed up on the Red Carpet or talking with Ellen and the two Jimmies on the talk show circuit we forget that those people are human. We do get a little glimpse of their humanness when they defy the rules of law and good taste and their booking photos show up on the covers of the supermarket tabloids.

If an actor or actress committed a crime or a sin in Old Hollywood, the studio's publicity machine went into action to keep it out of the media. There were fewer media when the newspapers and radio were kings. Coverups were easier in those days, when there were fewer ways to get the word out.

Then, along came television, the Internet, and the paparazzi. No place for the famous to hide their faces and transgressions anymore.

There is one major variable between idols and the rest of us. What they do for a living is seen by millions of people. The girl who bags your groceries and the guy who services your car do what they do for mere hundreds of people and no one gives it much thought. They are probably as good at their jobs as the actors and actresses are at theirs, yet we put the show biz people up there on pedestals. We love the famous. We want to *be* famous so we can live in a big house, drive an expensive car, be admired by the masses, and show them back home in Idaho that we are not the geek everyone thought we were in high school.

Then there is that element that craves mass attention to the extreme, but have no aptitude for getting famous through the front door. They're the ones who shoot up schools and churches, assassinate presidents, and become serial killers. They settle for infamy when fame eludes them.

Some who have no particular talent for the socially acceptable things that make a person famous are resigned—if not content—to bag the groceries, work behind the counter at the bank, spend a lifetime in a job where they do the same thing every day of their working lives. And they do it pretty much unnoticed.

I'll just keep watching my dead people.

THE AGE OF ENLIGHTENMENT

How many times when we were kids did we hear the words, "when you're older you will understand?"

Well, I'm just about as old as most people ever get and there's a lot of stuff I don't have a clue about.

When is this big flash of understanding supposed to hit me?

The question I always have when I hear one of those age qualifiers is: Yeah, but is there anything I can have or do right now?

When you're older you can get your driver's license, when you're older you can have a BB gun, when you're older you can . . . blah-blah-blah . . .

Waiting. It's what we spend a large part of our lives doing. Waiting for a bus, waiting in line, waiting for Christmas, waiting to be tall enough to get on the Ferris wheel by myself . . . yadda-yadda-yadda.

The things I *am* old enough for are no fun: arthritis, false teeth, hearing aids, canes . . . blah-blah-blah.

Senior discounts are nice, though. I started to get those when I was in my fifties. And I didn't even have to ask for them. Clerks just took one look at me and decided I was a senior.

Is that rude, or what? They could at least have had to decency to card me. They sure did that enough when I was a teenager and tried to buy beer.

One of these days I'll show all those people who told me to wait until I was older.

Just you wait.

123

THE SHAPE OF CARS

My wife says if they want to cut down on traffic they should take all the white cars off the road. It seems that every other car these days is white, including our own.

I have two ways I can tell ours from the herd in a supermarket parking lot. One is the design of the wheels. It's kind of a unique bunch of triangles. The other is by pressing the button on the remote and popping the trunk. When it rises I know I've got the right one.

Not only do a lot of cars have their color in common, most of them have everything else in common, too.

Back in "my day" cars were different from each other. A Chevy looked like a Chevy, a Ford like a Ford.

When I was about 12-years-old and my brother was three, my dad would take us to a spot that overlooked a main highway. As cars passed by my little brother would call out the names of the manufacturers. We were amazed that at only three-years-old he could distinguish a Ford from a Chevy from a Buick from a Hudson from a Packard from a Studebaker.

I defy anyone to accurately identify every car on the road today. Most of them don't even have the same names as when I was a kid. Some brands from the 1940s don't exist anymore: Studebaker, Hudson, Packard, Oldsmobile, Nash, Pontiac, Plymouth. Most of the traditional automakers that still have cars on the road have given them names of birds or wild animals or some word that doesn't seem to have any particular meaning.

I guess the automakers have focus groups that get together and toss words around that they think will appeal to the car-buying public: Spree, Fling, etc.

Well, listen up, General Motors. How about a Chevrolet "Goober?" I think a Ford "Swamp Rat" pickup truck would be pretty popular. I'm no focus group, but I think I have an eye and an ear for what would go over real big.

I can't tell you how many times I almost got into someone else's white car thinking it was my own, standing there pressing the clicker button and wondering why it didn't beep.

Once there was a strange woman in the car I was trying to get into. Well, she missed her chance, screaming like that.

Oh, that reminded me of another way I can locate my car from among all the other white ones in a supermarket parking lot; if my wife is in it.

I would recognize her almost immediately.

HUMAN NATURE VRS COMMON SENSE

It's strange what people can adapt themselves to; tornadoes, hurricanes, floods, mudslides, forest fires, earthquakes, Ford ownership—all manner of natural and man-made disasters.

Every time there is an earthquake in California, a lot of people move out of the state. Mostly, however, the people who live here patch up their injuries and properties and hunker down for the next one. Time passes and the population starts to increase again.

In a somewhat related human foible, where I come from originally there were typically two kinds of people: Ford people and Chevy people. The mechanic where I worked summers when I was still in high school used to say, "Chevys keep running with more things wrong with them than any other car." They rattled, groaned, and started on the coldest mornings, and they always seemed to get us there.

We were Chevy people and it was the 1950s.

The Ford people endured their overheating engines and faulty fuel pumps at that time and treated their auto frailties as just part of life. The Chevy people suffered the occasional gearshift locking up when they backed off the gas as they drove downhill, but that was a simple 60-second fix that anyone could do.

I suppose the Ford people got used to spending time in the dealer's service department waiting room and didn't know any other way. With some of those families, waiting rooms were a tradition; a place where their fellow sufferers gathered; an impromptu reunion of sorts.

Oh, there were the occasional Chrysler people, but nobody paid any attention to them. Let them deal with their unreliable transmissions and wheels that came off as they were driving down the road.

I can understand Mother Nature. It's Human Nature that baffles me sometimes.

In middle America, funnel clouds touch down and rip through enormous swaths. When the storm passes, residents come out of their storm cellars, pick themselves up and start all over again.

During World War II in Europe it was common for people whose homes had been bombed out to return to the rubble to live without walls and roofs.

All of which begs the question: Are we simply a really adaptable species or are we idiots?

I guess the pull of home and the force of habit are stronger than anything Ma Nature and fascist armies can throw at us.

That still doesn't completely explain why people kept buying Fords.

MISNAMING SMOKEY BEAR

With all the important issues troubling the world, one of my pet peeves probably should not hold a place of great weight.

But I need to at least go on record as having objected to the use of the word "the" in front of so many entities.

Like "Smokey *The* Bear." Nobody calls a human "John *The* Smith."

Smokey is a bear. Therefore, the proper form of referring to him is: "Smokey Bear."

That goes for the nation of Crimea. How many times have we heard about happenings in "*The* Crimea?" Nobody says "*The* Russia," which is Crimea's next door neighbor. Nobody says "*The* Alabama" or "*The* New York."

As my grandfather often said, "this is something up with which I will not put."

So spread the word all you members of the Language Police. "The" has no place in front of the names of bears, nations, states, or people.

If I have to go door-to-door to do it, I vow to reeducate every one of my fellow residents of the error of their ways here in *The* California.

DANGER LURKING IN THE GARDEN

Occasionally—just often enough to scare the bejeebies out of us—there will be a government announcement that some kind of food has been recalled because it has been found to be contaminated.

Beef is a common target. Eggs occasionally take the hit. Lettuce and spinach are frequently the alleged killer, especially the kind that comes in a sealed bag that acts as a little greenhouse where bugs can germinate.

We all grew up being told to eat our greens. Not to be confused with that green stuff way in the back of the refrigerator that has been there since the last ice age.

Then the government comes along and says this or that green may have a lethal bug in it.

Confusion time. Mom's voice is whispering in one ear the benefits of greenery and the government is screaming in the other ear that your Cesar, Greek or Cobb salad can kill you.

Moms are generally pretty reliable and, of course, the government never lies to us.

What's a poor consumer to do then? Well, we could just ignore the warnings and take our chances. We probably have better odds of surviving a salad than of winning the lottery. And, as far as we know, Ronald, Wendy, and Jack have always been straight with us.

Meanwhile, entire food service and agricultural industries are forced into ruin by the recalls of their products.

More people probably died taking selfies last year than from eating tainted food.

No one has ever backed off a cliff while munching on Romaine.

GENIUS AT WORK

One of the problems with living in a big city is that you rarely have any variety in the work you do. Everyone is a specialist, doing one small part of a large job. If an "on" switch has to be thrown, some labor union says one of their members has to do it. Someone else has to throw the "off" switch. That's the way it is in Metropolis.

I was in the radio and television business in Los Angeles (No, not repairing them). I would walk into a radio studio, sit down and read some news or commercial copy that someone else had written into a microphone operated by an engineer. A second engineer would operate the tape recorder and check the voice and music levels on a meter.

Before I moved to Los Angeles I got to be my own writer, engineer, producer, and announcer. Plus, I'd empty the waste baskets on my way out.

I grew tired of being a radio specialist in the big city and longed for the life of a general practitioner. When I moved back to my hometown for a few years in the late 1970s, I got to do it all.

I went to work for my small county weekly newspaper. One of the great joys of life for me in those days was that I not only found interesting stories, I got to write them, take the pictures, develop the negatives in those pre digital camera days, make the prints, and compose the pages of the issue.

That done I would drive the page "dummies" to the printer, wait while they were printed, bring the still-warm papers back to the newspaper office, and count out copies in preparation for me to deliver them to each news stand around the county.

For the first several months I worked for the newspaper I would count out the copies in segments of 25. When I got a stack of 100 I would tie them up with twine and write their destination on them. The trouble was, it took too long to count them out. Plus, if someone came by my work table and talked to me, my count would go haywire and I'd have to start over.

Well, after a couple of months of doing it that way it dawned on me that, if 100 newspapers weighed a certain amount once, they should weigh the same the next time.

I found an unused scale and, by golly, it worked out. The job that used to take me an hour-and-a-half now took me about 40 minutes.

My next project was going to be to figure out a way to get those heavy bales of newspapers into the truck with less effort.

I admit to being a little slow at figuring out that aspect of the project. Probably because I was kind of new at the genius business.

MORE QUESTIONS THAN ANSWERS

Why is it that the cost of a gallon of gas at a gas station is X number of dollars and cents—plus nine-tenths of a cent? Why is that fraction always at the end of the price? I'm charged the full cent, since there is no nine-tenths-of-a-cent U.S. coin.

Notice I didn't refer to those establishments as "service" stations? Service at gas stations long ago went the way of the nickel candy bar, 15-cent theater admission, and holding onto the girl while dancing. If you want your windshield washed and your oil checked, you have to do it yourself.

While we're taking on the petroleum industry, consider this: why is it that the signs at gas stations always give the price and the word "unleaded" after it? *All* gas sold for cars in this country is unleaded, why bother to spell it out on the sign?

Is it the oil company's way of saying "we are no longer putting lead in our gas, so we are charging you extra for not doing it?" Similar to the dairy industry's removing cream from milk, and charging you more for the low-fat option. Then they take the fat they removed from the milk, make butter and cheese out of it, and charge you premium prices for what should have been yours in the first place.

When Col. Harland Sanders sold his Kentucky Fried Chicken business to a group of investors, the KFC originator became unhappy with some of the cost-cutting changes the new owners made. Sanders complained loudly and publically that the mashed potatoes and gravy now resembled "library paste." He further alleged that they had apparently cut out some of the 11 "secret" spices KFC was known for.

Another case of consumers getting "less for more."

The owners shut the old man up by restoring at least some of the original KFC recipe ingredients and paying him to actively promote the brand.

Soap companies once sold a product called: "soap." The size and shape of a bar of "soap" was pretty uniform throughout the industry and much of it had a harsh or medicinal smell to it. Then some company executive came up with the idea of adding perfume, making that bar convex on one side and concave on the other, marketing it as being artfully contoured to the human body, renaming it a "beauty bar," and—charging you more for it.

It seems to me that every time I get an answer to a troubling question, the answer presents more questions.

All I know for sure is that for every ten gallons of gas I buy, somebody owes me a penny.

ANOTHER SIGN OF AGING

A lot of us retired guys have plenty of free time on our hands. Unlike a hundred years ago when I was a kid, free time doesn't get us in as much trouble these days. They say, "Idle hands are the devil's workshop." Well, the devil has to work harder these days because we have learned many ways to avoid getting caught at our kind of mischief.

I kind of identify with Earl, in the "Pickles" cartoon. He and another old guy are often sitting on a park bench in conversation, grumbling about this or that.

My friends and I have our own favorite grumbling venues.

Interesting how conversation has changed over the years. When we were young the topics could be put into three distinct categories. In fact, I once took a note pad and pencil on one of our teen outings and dissected our conversational topics. We alternated between Sports, Cars, and "Women." We didn't know much about women at that stage of our lives, but we but spoke on the subject with expertise nevertheless. You can probably guess which topic was the main one.

Nowadays, the topics center around the state of our health, the number of pills we're taking, which friends of ours have "dropped dead of nothing" at 90, and how much farther it is down to the mailbox than it used to be.

It's true. Just a few years ago the mailbox at the road was about a hundred yards away. Now—without having moved an inch from this very spot—it seems about a mile-and-a-half.

Remember those TV ads where the woman is lying on the floor and she says, "I've fallen and I can't get up?" Well, I haven't quite gotten to that stage, but I do consider carefully whether I will pick up something I have dropped.

There was a time when I would dive to the ground to pick up a lost penny. Now it would have to be a much larger denomination for me to bend down there.

I think I'm up to a quarter now.

LOOKING FOR A CURE

People who are trying to quit smoking cigarettes have many aids to help them kick the habit: nicotine patches and gum, self-help books, support groups, nagging spouses.

But what about those of us who are addicted to, say, ice cream?

There is no ice cream patch. If there were it would be pretty messy.

Like Pavlov's dog, my mouth begins to water when I hear the ice cream truck's song as it cruises neighborhoods in its unholy quest to get the very young hooked.

I suppose it could be worse. If ice cream were outlawed there would be many more addicts. That's what happened when a Constitutional amendment banned alcohol.

There is a law of nature that says that if you can't have a thing, then that is the very thing you will want. It also works that way with the "must-have" toy around Christmastime every year. Word gets out that a toy is in short supply and that your kid will be scorned by his and her peers if you don't stand in line at the local toy store to get one for him or her. Meanwhile, he and she are at home crying their eyes out because he or she will be pariahs if he or she doesn't get one of the rare thingamabobs for his or her very own.

People got violent when the Cabbage Patch dolls and Tickle Me Elmo toys were hard to find. Fights broke out at toy stores. Pet Rock sales really took off when the rumor started that they were only a few left. Prices soared and a black market developed for each of those items.

Bad enough if consuming ice cream were a *crime*. What if churches declared it a *sin*? That would be the cherry on top, so to speak. There would surely be a run on the stuff. Most ice cream addicts would do their sinning out of town, of course. Either that or at small back room ice cream parlors where, if you had the right connections, you could feed your addiction.

Organized crime would again flourish, supplying the illicit product to eager scofflaws. Modern-day Elliot Nesses would be combing the land for modern-day Al Capones. Shady characters would lure people into dark alleys to sell fudge ripple out of the trunks of their cars.

Those deprived of their ice cream would be lying in dark rooms, pleading pathetically for butter pecan, French vanilla—their mothers.

Families would be ripped apart. America's already-overcrowded prisons could not accommodate the enormous influx.

Fortunately I have my own ice cream maker and a large freezer.

The only way you will get my ice cream away from me is if you pry it from my cold, dead fingers.

THANKS

Special thanks to all who contributed to the creation of this book of random thoughts of a disturbed mind.

To Phawnda Moore and Ron Greenwood for suggestions as to how a sow's ear might more closely resemble a silk purse. Thanks anyway.

To author and friend Gloria Nagy-Wurman, and longtime friend Bobbi Maas-Weinstein for urging me to turn a blog into a book.

Made in the USA
Middletown, DE
30 January 2019